# STORYTELLING
## WITH PURPOSE

**Digital Projects to
Ignite Student Curiosity**

Michael Hernandez

**International Society for Technology in Education**
**ARLINGTON, VIRGINIA**

"Michael Hernandez's new book on digital storytelling is a must-have for educators. It's a clear, practical guide for infusing storytelling in any subject. Hernandez outlines the essentials of digital storytelling with easy-to-follow steps and relevant examples. This book is perfect for teachers aiming to integrate more multimedia into their lessons and empower their students as creators. It's an invaluable resource for enhancing classroom engagement and creativity."

**Monica Burns, Ed.D.**
**author of *EdTech Essentials* and founder of ClassTechTips.com**

"Michael Hernandez is a master storyteller and a master teacher, and this beautifully designed book is a perfect example of his craft. Through the range of practical ideas and the illustrative examples in *Storytelling With Purpose*, every teacher, storyteller, and creator who aspires to refine their approaches will benefit from engaging with Michael's latest work. This is one of those rare books where you can benefit from reading it linearly from front to back or jump around to the areas that interest you the most (at first— you'll be compelled to read it all no matter what!). This is a wonderful contribution to the body of literature that focuses on purposeful, student-centered education."

**Dr. Reshan Richards**
**Lecturer, Columbia University School of Professional Studies**
**Co-Founder, Explain Everything (acquired by Promethean, Inc.)**

"*Storytelling with Purpose* is a much-needed resource for today's educator. Through stories and examples from his experience as a teacher, Michael brings us on a journey to understand ways to support storytelling in the classroom and to empower the voices of youth by design. Readers are able to explore different types, forms, and purposes of digital stories and then are guided through a creation process positioning students (and teachers) as thoughtful observers of the world, creators of stories, and messengers of perspective, experience, and action. Inspiring and inventive, this book will be one I can return to again and again!"

**Jennifer Williams**
**ISTE Author, Global Educator**
**Co-founder Take Action Global and TeachSDGs**

"The entire experience in Michael's classes set me on a course through college and into my journalism career, where I still lean on all those lessons every day."

**Alicia Hastey**
**Producer, *CBS Evening News* with Norah O'Donnell**

"Michael is an individual with a superb understanding of how to adapt to a student's comprehension of material. He not only has the 'know how' but he is able to convey his message so that it's suitable to the listener. He can teach anyone!"

**Hunter Isbell**
**Curriculum Director and Music Teacher**

"We value his ability to integrate his classroom experience with his extensive knowledge of tech and its power to personalize learning for students of all ages. He is an exceptional storyteller and talented speaker."

**Kathy Crowley**
**Founder, Readability Matters**

# STORYTELLING WITH PURPOSE

Digital Projects to Ignite Student Curiosity

Michael Hernandez

Director of Books and Journals: *Emily Reed*
Senior Acquisitions Editor: *Valerie Witte*
Editor: *Stephanie Argy*
Copy Editor: *Lisa Hein*
Proofreader: *Emily Padgett*
Indexer: *Kento Ikeda*
Book Design and Production: *Danielle Foster*
Cover Design: *Edwin Ouellette*

Library of Congress Cataloging-in-Publication Data

Names: Hernandez, Michael (Educator), author.
Title: Storytelling with purpose : digital projects to ignite student
  curiosity / Michael Hernandez.
Description: First edition. | Portland, Oregon : International Society for
  Technology in Education, 2023. | Includes bibliographical references and
  index.
Identifiers: LCCN 2023028827 (print) | LCCN 2023028828 (ebook) | ISBN
  9781564849960 (paperback) | ISBN 9781564849977 (epub) | ISBN
  9781564849984 (pdf)
Subjects: LCSH: Digital storytelling. | Project method in teaching.
Classification: LCC LB1042 .H47 2023  (print) | LCC LB1042  (ebook) | DDC
  371.3/6--dc23/eng/20231012
LC record available at https://lccn.loc.gov/2023028827
LC ebook record available at https://lccn.loc.gov/2023028828

First Edition
ISBN: 978-1-56484-996-0

Ebook version available
ISBN EPUB: 978-1-56484-997-7
ISBN PDF: 978-1-56484-998-4

Printed in the United States of America

ISTE® is a registered trademark of the International Society for Technology in Education.

# About ISTE

The International Society for Technology in Education (ISTE) is home to a passionate community of global educators who believe in the power of technology to transform teaching and learning, accelerate innovation and solve tough problems in education.

ISTE inspires the creation of solutions and connections that improve opportunities for all learners by delivering: practical guidance, evidence-based professional learning, virtual networks, thought-provoking events and the ISTE Standards. ISTE is also the leading publisher of books focused on technology in education. For more information or to become an ISTE member, visit iste.org. Subscribe to ISTE's YouTube channel and connect with ISTE on X (formerly Twitter), Facebook and LinkedIn.

## Related ISTE Titles

*Moviemaking in the Classroom: Lifting Student Voices Through Digital Storytelling* by Jessica Pack (2021)

*Teach Boldly: Using Edtech for Social Good* by Jennifer Williams (2019)

*New Realms for Writing: Inspire Student Expression with Digital Age Formats* by Michele Haiken (2019)

*Bring History and Civics to Life: Lessons and Strategies to Cultivate Informed, Empathetic Citizens* by Karalee Wong Nakatsuka and Laurel Aguilar-Kirchhoff (2022)

To see all books available from ISTE, please visit iste.org/books.

# About the Author

Always a slow reader and a perennial bad speller, Michael struggled to appreciate books and writing growing up. It was an unpleasant chore to read and write, which created a disconnect between incredible ideas and inspiring stories, and Michael's ability to access or write them himself. As he collected graphic novels, he began to understand the connection between art, design, and story. Then, on his 11th birthday, he received a storytelling tool that he had been begging for for years, and that would ultimately change his life: a 35mm camera. But in school, the only stories that mattered, that were considered serious and worthy of attention and praise, were printed with text.

Then in college, Michael saw his first arthouse films and was struck with the realization that cinema could be much more than a populist distraction. It was, in the right hands, a form of literature on par with the greatest novels. His love of cinema took him to film school, where he also began teaching as a graduate student. It turned out that this, too, was a form of storytelling, one that had the potential to evoke emotion, spark conversations, and empower individuals to become their best selves. The path to teaching revealed itself through storytelling, and Michael embraced his role encouraging young people to tell stories that matter.

Since taking the leap into education, Michael has become an award-winning teacher, international speaker, author, and curriculum designer who helps individuals and organizations discover and share authentic stories that matter. He has been featured by *Forbes*, Edutopia, PBS, NPR, and SXSW EDU. Some of his most memorable teaching experiences include moderating conversations with Ken Burns and Dolores Huerta, and teaching his daughter Maya, who was one of his high school journalism students.

As a trusted expert, he has worked with schools, tech startups, nonprofits, and corporations to develop their brand and engage their stakeholders. His clients include Apple, Adobe, Google, and National Geographic. *Change The Narrative*, his podcast and monthly newsletter, has a global audience of thousands.

Michael is an Apple Distinguished Educator, PBS Digital Innovator, and National Geographic Grosvenor Teacher Fellow. Follow him on these social platforms:

Instagram: @Changing.The.Narrative
X/Twitter: @cinehead
LinkedIn: bit.ly/MichaelHernandezLinkedIn

# Acknowledgments

## Publisher Acknowledgments

ISTE gratefully acknowledges the contributions of the following:

ISTE Standards Reviewers: Laurie Guyon, Kristy Nelson, Tiffany Rexhausen, Gaby Richard-Harrington

Manuscript Reviewers: Conni Burke-Mulligan, Julie Jaeger, Krishna R. Millsapp, Amanda Nguyen, Jessica Shupik

## Author Acknowledgments

Everyone owes a debt to their teachers for helping us become the people we are today. Their passion, personality, and philosophy live on through us, and in turn, our own students. To my fourth-grade teacher, Mrs. Baird, for teaching me about ions and wrinkles in time. To my fifth- and sixth-grade teacher, Mr. Mattos, for the many creative projects, computer code, Kahlil Gibran, and *Cosmos*. To Mr. Ratcliffe for teaching me about science in one explosive class period. To my undergraduate mentor, Dr. Stephen Lee, for bonding over *Northern Exposure* and the Sex Pistols (on vinyl) and introducing me to mind-blowing cinema (Chris Marker! Luis Bunuel!). To Dr. Sue Scheibler, my graduate school mentor—and probably the smartest person I know—who subjected me to double features of Andrei "You Call This a Movie?" Tarkovsky, wrote original poetry for my thesis film, and served as a judge for my own students' film festival for nearly 20 years.

Much love to my global Apple Distinguished Educators family who opened my mind to new possibilities in teaching and continually serve as a sounding board and inspiration for work and life: Kurt and Christine Klynen, Cathy Hunt, Keri-Lee Beasley, Mary Kemper, Eoin Hughes, Erika Moser, Antonio Manriquez, Nancy Kawaja, Michelle Cordy, Sharon Drummond, Maxx Judd, Matt Baier, Marco Torres, and those who appear in this book: Dan Ryder, Karrin Burns, Jodie Deinhammer, Leah Lacrosse, and Karen Bosch.

Thanks to my learning community around the world who make me smarter, wiser, and easier to get along with: Dr. Monica Burns, Dr. Jennifer Williams, Michelle Moore, Ben Walker, Dave Davis, Luis Perez, Greg Alchin, Ellen Austin, Brendan Constantine, and my writer's group who got me through this book, one 7:00 a.m. meeting at a time: Ela Ben-Ur, Julia Kramer, Susie Wise, Jill Vialet, Juliette Melton, and Erin Huizenga.

And cheers to those who inspire my soul: Jonathan Gold, Wong Kar-Wai, James Baldwin, McCoy Tyner, Gustav Mahler, and Annie Dillard.

## Dedication

For my parents, Juan and Claudia, lifelong educators who were my first teachers, and from whom I continue to learn every day. For my daughter, Maya, who inspires me with her creativity and passion, and who taught me how to be a better teacher.

# CONTENTS

Contents

# Contents

# PROLOGUE

*"If you want to build a ship, don't drum up people to collect wood and don't assign them tasks and work, but rather teach them to long for the endless immensity of the sea."*

**—Antoine de Saint-Exupéry, author of *The Little Prince*.**

For 25 years, I've taught high school journalism, cinematic arts, and photography. While these courses have been frequently relegated to the margins as "elective" by standardized test companies and academic traditionalists, we are realizing now that storytelling is in fact central to learning and plays a crucial role in finding solutions to some of our most pressing challenges in education and society.

The COVID-19 pandemic shone a light on the flaws of traditional learning methods, both in terms of their effectiveness and the willingness of both students and teachers to play the game of direct instruction/memorization/regurgitation, which often only serves privileged students (CEW Georgetown University, 2019). We struggled to give ourselves and our students a good reason why school (in-person or remote) was important. Suddenly, everyone had new clarity on what mattered most to them, their lives, and the good of the planet, and school often wasn't part of that.

Cyberbullying, trolling, misinformation, and disinformation campaigns spun by bad actors on digital and traditional media platforms have fanned the flames of racism and hate and led to insurrections and violence around the world. The promise that social media and digital storytelling once held as a democratizing force for sharing information and ideas has been tarnished, and many parents and educators have reacted by banning technology, hoping that if we don't see social media, it doesn't exist and neither will its potential downsides. But this stance to embrace digital illiteracy under the guise of protecting our kids has only backfired. It makes teachers less legitimate in the eyes of our students, leaving them vulnerable to those who are more digitally savvy and antagonistic, and creates a generation of citizens who are unprepared to navigate the political, cultural, and professional world that has been digital-first for decades.

Advances in artificial intelligence now allow anyone to prompt an app to quickly write essays, college application letters, curriculum, computer code, or anything else you request. Suddenly, educators are forced to question what we're teaching and why, and if we haven't already, ask the most fundamental question of all: What do we mean by "learning"? Is it just teaching kids the mechanics of how to communicate ideas (grammar, spelling, sentence structure—all now rendered pointless by AI) or is it about focusing on the purpose of learning? And how can our students make good, ethical decisions when no one is looking?

This book is an attempt to answer these existential challenges by reframing the learning process as one based on empowerment, centering student curiosity, purpose, and joy as the engines that drive all learning experiences. Using nonfiction storytelling as a framework for learning embraces the idea that learning should be an authentic experience, both in the academic sense of leveraging integrity to conduct research and develop ideas, as well as with the ultimate motivating goal of creating an original product that will have an impact on an audience beyond the classroom. Digital storytelling can be the framework upon which we hang our curriculum (skills, knowledge, information) and an opportunity to help students develop a more positive relationship to learning within the context of a global society.

My experience as a secondary teacher and as a dad has revealed that many students and teachers perceive curiosity and wonder as a weakness—a source of anxiety for many students who may fear getting a bad grade or looking unintelligent because of their lack of understanding or knowledge. We have also become a society where many take offense when our assumptions or the status quo are challenged, making it difficult to embrace inquiry in the classroom and beyond. This book offers ways to flip that model around and honors and embraces student curiosity as the driving force behind learning. Instead of being punished for what we don't know (through grades, personal status, scholarships, honor roll, etc.), we elevate and praise the most interesting, provocative questions and the extent to which we answer them.

My goal for this book is to help all stakeholders adopt a new set of mindsets, including learning to:

◆ understand how students can use nonfiction storytelling as a way of thinking and processing information

◆ use storytelling as a vehicle for inquiry and assessment, not as entertainment or distraction

◆ encourage student-centered learning where teachers are leaders/facilitators

◆ use multimedia as an effective, relevant way to communicate ideas beyond text alone

◆ integrate nonfiction storytelling projects in classrooms of all grade levels and subject areas

◆ honor and support student independence, ownership, and personal responsibility within the context of a global society

◆ reimagine what we mean by "learning" and "success" as human-centered experiences rather than data-driven processes

## Not a "Nice-to-Have": Storytelling as an Essential Skill for Learning

While it's true that school can't be a free-for-all where students do whatever they want by choosing only what "feels good" to study and leaving behind essential skills and experiences, it's also true that traditional curriculum and teaching methods, under added pressure of high stakes testing and "accountability," have left our students unprepared to be successful citizens in a contemporary world (Marciano, 2001).

Storytelling projects are often treated as a reward for students once their "real work" has been completed. Somehow we've developed a mindset that project-based learning experiences like nonfiction storytelling are a lower form of learning than traditional assignments, perhaps because they can be fun and rewarding, rather than tedious or painful. But rigor and hard work can be synonymous with passion and purpose—we can and should enjoy working hard to achieve goals that are meaningful and for causes we care about. This is really the most important lesson we need to teach our students.

For nearly a quarter century, I've witnessed the power of storytelling projects to elevate learning and invigorate students' sense of curiosity and provide meaning and purpose for school. But don't take my word for it. There is a ton of research that supports my anecdotal experience and verifies storytelling and its associated skills and learning experiences as effective ways to elevate learning across disciplines and grade levels.

Some of the research finds:

✦ Storytelling is an effective way to improve literacy (Miller & Pennycuff, 2008).

✦ Curiosity improves reading and math achievement (Shah et al., 2018).

✦ Curiosity is a basic element of cognition and even to our biology (Kidd & Hayden, 2015).

✦ Image-based content, alongside text-based content, may serve as an effective pedagogical supplement to students with or without cognitive disabilities (Smith et al., 2021).

✦ Creative activities result in job mastery and control and positive performance-related outcomes (Eschleman et al., 2014).

✦ Memorization of facts (like for quizzes and tests) does not help higher-level thinking, but that retrieval experiences—like those required for storytelling projects—do (Agarwal, 2019).

# How to Use This Book

This book provides practical examples and classroom-tested advice to get teachers started with digital storytelling projects, no matter your resources or technical expertise. I recognize that trying something new can be scary or difficult unless you have the support of colleagues, administration, and parents. To help you on your journey, I've also included research, examples from my classroom, and testimony from teachers across the country that show how the ideas in this book can help solve real, day-to-day challenges that educators face. It's my hope that this book can help make the case to stakeholders in your community for moving to a more learner-centered pedagogy based on authenticity and inquiry, and an understanding that a rigorous education should also be one filled with purpose and joy.

The book is divided into three parts, the What, Why, and How of digital storytelling:

✦ Part I defines what digital storytelling is and how its unique capabilities can elevate learning for students of all abilities. I break down the steps of the storytelling process, share secrets about working collaboratively, and tell how to come up with good story ideas.

- ✦ Part II is dedicated to understanding why we should use digital story projects, and how they fit naturally into our existing curriculum, including how to use them for inquiry and design thinking, and as a way to provide authentic, uncheatable assessments.

- ✦ Part III is a compilation of my favorite storytelling projects, organized by learning needs, like anthologies, observation and inquiry, creativity, and writing. I've included simple, easy projects you can use right away, as well as advice for more complex projects when you and your students are ready.

- ✦ The appendices are a curated set of resources to help you find the best tools to use for story projects, ethical guidance about copyright and privacy, and a bibliography of my favorite books, organizations, and resources.

If you can't wait to start creating digital stories, jump ahead to chapter 16 for Quick Win projects you can use with your students right away, then circle back to earlier chapters for advice on assessment, developing story ideas, and the logistics of how to integrate these projects into your curriculum.

The ideas and mindsets I describe are intended to help students in your school become curious, confident, engaged citizens who have a healthy relationship to learning throughout their lives. But this book is just the beginning.

## Digital Resources: Student Examples and Updated Tools

Digital tools and resources evolve rapidly, so I've created a website that collects my latest, updated recommendations for tools, articles, and other resources for your classroom. You can also see examples of the student projects discussed in this book.

Scan the QR code to access the site.

Join a global community of educators who share a common goal of creating authentic learning experiences by sharing your ideas, student projects, and insights by using the hashtag #StorytellingWithPurpose. Have questions or need advice on how to use these ideas in your learning space? Visit storytelling-with-purpose.com or drop me an email: michael@storytelling-with-purpose.com

## PART I

# WHAT ARE DIGITAL STORIES?

Digital stories are much more than videos—they include a broad range of interactive multimedia formats, like infographics, audio recordings, photographs, and digital books that are flexible enough to be used in every subject area and grade level. In this first part of the book, I talk about what digital storytelling can be, how it amplifies and expands on what teachers already do best, and share the secrets of how to create effective stories.

# CHAPTER 1
# ELEMENTS OF DIGITAL STORIES

What are digital stories, and why would teachers want to use them in the classroom? This chapter shows how the unique features of digital storytelling can open possibilities for how students relate to ideas and information and discusses how the dynamic nature of digital stories changes the relationship between author and audience to create a more equitable, personalized learning experience for people of all abilities and backgrounds.

## Interactivity

Textbooks, novels, and manuals are designed as a one-way transmission of information, mirroring a traditional mindset about education: students as vessels to be filled with information from books and lectures. But direct instruction can lead to lower engagement by neglecting students' sense of curiosity and discouraging ownership of learning. The interactivity made possible with digital stories doesn't necessarily change the information or content, but rather changes how authors and audiences relate to that information.

Digital stories transform narratives into a participatory experience by:

+ providing the ability to review multimedia at different speeds to enhance understanding

+ zooming in on images for better analysis

+ interacting with the audience via comment threads

+ collaborative authorship and global distribution stories (via cloud storage, or links posted on social media, websites, and audience re-sharing)

## Hyperlinks

Where analog stories are closed and often linear, digital stories are open and non-linear. Links placed in digital books, blogs, websites, and social media stories allow audiences to navigate between sections within a single story or to resources related to but outside of a story. This lets audiences create their own learning adventure, which makes for a more robust and personalized experience. And the ability to rewind, replay, or skip through a story honors the audience's unique learning needs, time constraints, and reading conditions.

Hyperlinks allow many advantages for student authors, including:

- connecting stories to primary source documentation (like a live footnote)
- making it easier for audiences to extend learning through further exploration
- keeping stories evergreen and up-to-date by linking to sites with the latest scientific, artistic, journalistic, and cultural information

This is also a great opportunity to discuss hyperlink literacy and the purpose of curation. Like the recommended resources at the end of this book, hyperlinks offer a way for students to thoughtfully add knowledge and provide context for their stories. This leads to important discussions about the quality and reliability of sources they use and positions student authors as trusted experts who can recommend sources and provide the audience opportunities for future study of a topic.

## Audience as Coauthor of Stories

Just as we reread passages of an article that we need to understand better or jump around a magazine or newspaper in a non-linear way, digital stories enable the audience to leap to different sections of a website or digital book, skip to the most recent podcast episode, or review the most important sections of a YouTube video. Commenting features of publicly posted work can create a dialogue between audience and author that creates an extended meta-story with the potential to add new perspectives and clarity not possible with a single author's perspective. (See how this affected one of my students in chapter 9.)

## Multimedia

Multimedia—content other than text, such as images, video, or audio—helps student authors and their audiences understand ideas and information in ways that text can't, such as providing evidence, creating context, revealing relationships, and designing visual metaphors.

**Show, don't tell:** photos and video assist scientists, mathematicians, and journalists by documenting the world with concrete visual evidence and material for analysis.

**Clarity and context:** photographs, video, and illustrations describe complex concepts, while maps and data visualizations reveal patterns and spatial relationships.

**Experiential learning:** creating multimedia artifacts often requires students to engage with other people, places, and events beyond the classroom, creating opportunities to build interpersonal skills and develop a personal relationship to the curriculum.

*Find out more about how to use the unique traits of multimedia in chapter 2.*

## Shareability

When stories are shared with an audience other than the teacher, it helps students see a purpose for their work, because they know it won't just end up in the trash. In fact, their story can even help or inspire others. This is instrumental in unlocking student engagement.

It's also an opportunity to talk about our responsibility as storytellers. Some of the most profound learning happens when my students grapple with the relationship between themselves and their audience, including:

✦ choices about how to craft the most effective story

✦ concern for how their work might impact others

✦ discovering personal and cultural biases (which stories get told or left untold)

## Low Cost

Using free or low-cost digital storytelling tools helps schools save money and have less impact on the environment. Buying, printing, storing, and shipping traditional materials isn't an option for many schools, and distribution of stories via social media, websites, email, or cloud storage can help reach global audiences in minutes. Updates to stories that include the latest data or other information can be done instantly, without having to reprint and redistribute, as with traditional publishing.

## Accessibility, Equity, and Inclusion

A ramp at a sidewalk helps parents with strollers, the elderly, and people with injuries get over the curb—not just people in a wheelchair. In the same way, our assignments, in the form of digital storytelling, help all learners access our curriculum. The concept of Universal Design for Learning (UDL) embodies this idea by recognizing that accessibility features benefit all learners, not just those with diagnosed disabilities.

Consider how student-created digital stories can help us assess all students in more equitable ways: instead of being tripped up by the assessment tool or process, students have the flexibility to demonstrate their knowledge and application of that knowledge in ways that suit them best. Written assignments, for example, may hinder students who are language learners or those with learning disabilities, and timed tests may get in the way of any student who processes and works at different speeds.

The unique features of digital stories, including speech to text, text to speech, the ability to adjust font size and line spacing, and closed-captioning for videos, increase fluency for all learners (Crowley & Jordan, 2019) and make our classrooms more inclusive. The ability to literally show what you know through photography, video, audio, and performance elevates our ability to accurately check student understanding through multiple metrics and pathways.

Just to be clear, this isn't about making exceptions or easier assignments (creating an effective documentary is much harder and more complex than writing a report!). This is about students owning their learning and our respect for them as responsible individuals within our learning communities.

# Multimodal Literacy

Multimodal literacy is the concept that students develop the ability to understand and create "texts" that use a variety of media—such as video, photography, sound, gestures, etc. Posters, for example, use the modes of text, image, and color to convey ideas. Social media memes are a modern take on posters, because they also include cultural references and humor that often rely on irony and hyperbole. Video is inherently multimodal, intertwining photography, sound, movement, editing, performance, and dialogue.

Developing multimodal literacy is vital for developing media-literate students who can communicate in the world outside of school. (Kalantzis, 2016). It's also a great opportunity for our students to check their assumptions about the best ways to learn and communicate knowledge.

*FIGURE 1.1* **Seeing Sound:** *Multimedia allows students of all abilities to access our curriculum and be included. In one case, my deaf and hard of hearing students used audio waveforms (visualized sound levels) to guide their editing of video projects. Their edits turned out to be more precise than their hearing classmates, which boosted their confidence and allowed them to participate fully in the class.*

# CHAPTER 2

# BEYOND WORDS: THE POWER OF MULTIMEDIA STORYTELLING

When we say, "Oh, I see!" what we really mean is that we understand. But the metaphor of sight as knowledge is more than just a turn of phrase—seeing *is* believing, and digital stories offer opportunities to use our senses to make sense of the world and to learn in three dimensions.

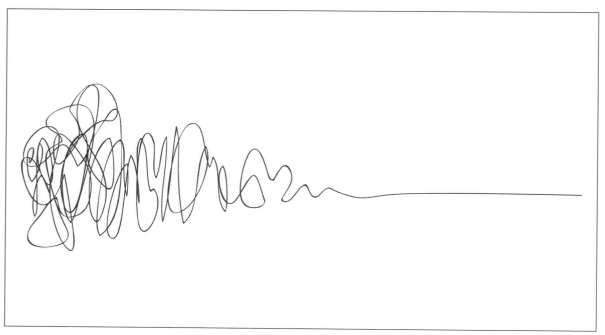

**FIGURE 2.1** *The creative process. Even a simple line can convey complicated processes and help an audience understand without the need for words. Source: The Process of Design Squiggle by Damien Newman, thedesignsquiggle.com*

Consider the ironic humor of a political cartoon, the way a time-lapse video spans seasons or the lifetime of a plant, and how audio reveals the song of humans and the natural world. Illustrations aren't just for assembling IKEA furniture—they're critical for assembling knowledge, especially concepts too complex for words. (We'd literally be lost without maps and charts, for example.) So why have we privileged the written word when multimedia has so much to offer?

While writing is at the heart of every digital story (think scripts, interview questions, captions), I like to think of multimedia as a different kind of writing, with its own grammar, that works alongside words to create spatial relationships and provide unique information and detail that words simply can't.

In this chapter, I share the secrets of using multimedia (photography, audio, video, data visualizations, and illustrations) to provide clarity, improve accessibility, and tell stories that resonate with an audience's heart and mind.

## Photography: A Thousand Words

Photography is the most familiar and accessible type of visual storytelling. It's also a powerful way to document reality and provide visual evidence, making it a great place to start when creating multimedia stories.

### Photography as Nonfiction Storytelling

Historians, journalists, and scientists rely on the collection of information to understand events, draw conclusions, and make predictions about the future.

## What Photography Brings to Storytelling

**Visual evidence.** Documents an event, action, or phenomenon.

**Context.** Shows the relationship between objects or people within an environment.

**Freezing action.** Allows detailed analysis of an object or action that's not possible when experiencing it live or while in motion.

**FIGURE 2.2** *Eadweard Muybridge, Animal Locomotion, Plate 626, 1887. Using photography to freeze movement of animals and people, Muybridge was able to analyze physical phenomena, like the galloping horse in this image, which revealed for the first time that the animals leave the ground while running.*

Photography is a great way to document phenomena and provide proof—or visual evidence—to support research and persuasive stories alike.

## Photography for Analysis

In the 1800s, Eadweard Muybridge created the first stop-motion images, which proved the power of photography to aid scientific research by analyzing movement. His images were the first evidence that horses left the ground briefly while running, which had previously been impossible to observe with the naked eye. Consider using photographs in the same way to freeze movement to analyze details students might not be physically able to perceive on their own, or use them to create time for closer inspection and reflection.

Macro and telephoto lenses, like microscopes and telescopes, can help us observe details of objects up close or far away, and capturing people's faces can also provide an emotional, human dimension to a story, an important qualitative type of data collection.

## Audio: Storytelling with Emotion

Audio is an underestimated and immersive storytelling medium that is also one of the least complicated to create. Without being bogged down with visual skills like composition and lighting that are required for video and photography, these types of stories allow students to focus on elements like writing, speaking, and conducting interviews.

Sonic stories tend to be the best at capturing emotion because they're an intimate and personal medium. Consider someone's accent or the fatigue in their voice, or the specific sounds of a frozen lake beginning to melt. Unlike photography and video, audio stories can also minimize audience

## What Audio Brings to Storytelling

**Details.** Animal calls in nature, the power of thunder, the strength of a rushing river, congestion of traffic on a street, accents of regional and foreign languages, the sounds of machines when they work right or when they are malfunctioning all can establish atmosphere and a sense of place, which help us feel what it's like to be in a particular place. Accents can tell us where someone is from.

**Emotion and tone.** Vocal tone may reveal someone's emotional state or if they're being hyperbolic, sarcastic, or ironic.

**Music.** Whether captured intrinsically as part of a recording, like a band or radio playing in the background during an interview, or added on top of a story later, like a film score, music can evoke emotion, create motifs, and provide opportunities for allusion. It's also a great way to document and examine culture and history.

**Accessibility.** The ability to record and playback ideas without the need for text puts the focus back on content and thinking and removes technical and physical obstacles of reading and writing. For younger students whose ideas may surpass their writing ability, those with learning disabilities, and students with mobility issues that make writing or typing difficult, consider recording student voices as an alternative to written assignments.

bias: because we can't see the people being interviewed, audiences are less liable to judge them based on race, age, or how they're dressed.

# Oral Histories

Audio histories have long been used by sociologists and anthropologists to document people and culture. StoryCorps is a nonprofit that produces audio histories by letting people record a personal story in a mobile recording studio. These stories are later archived at the Library of Congress's American Folklife Center. They also provide resources and a mobile app to help you record and upload your own audio histories. See ideas for oral history projects in chapter 12.

Use audio stories to collect data and information, such as:

+ eyewitness accounts of historical events
+ sounds of the natural world like animal calls and weather
+ music, languages, and regional accents that are quickly disappearing in our globalized world (cultural phenomena)
+ conversations when studying foreign languages

## Audio Stories for Research

Sound is a powerful tool for both qualitative and quantitative research. Interviewing experts and eye-witnesses helps students and their audiences make personal connections to topics and build empathy for others because we hear evidence and reactions directly from a real stakeholder. Documenting the sounds of a phenomenon or event provides context, data, and evidence. Consider documenting the sounds of your community and use audio stories for research, analysis, and preservation.

## Quantitative research

Audio recordings can collect data in two ways: inside the content of the recording, and data from the recording itself.

Data inside the content of the recording comes from decoding statements from people who might be interviewed in a story, such as experts and stakeholders who share statistics and other countable info. This might include the number of times someone has won or lost a sports game, how many siblings they have, how many books they've read, or what countries they've immigrated from. Experts can provide data related to story topics, such as population changes in your town, the cost of repairing cities after large storms, or distances in migration patterns.

Data derived from the recording itself can provide unique insights about the topic, too. For example, counting the frequency that something happens over a period of time, like the number of times a woodpecker pecks wood (slow down the recording to count!), the number of cars passing in a specific location on a road, or the frequency of certain words used in a conversation. Duration can also be a data point, such as the time it takes for vehicles to pass or the sustain of a musical note.

## Video: Sculpting in Time

Video combines the visual evidence of photography with the emotional detail of audio and adds a new dimension that makes the medium unique: movement. Whereas photography freezes action, video shines when it's used to show movement and change. The use of slow motion, frame-by-frame playback, and time-lapse videography can help students analyze actions more closely to reveal details not possible with the naked eye or photography alone. It's also the medium that best helps audiences feel what it's like to be in a specific place and time.

## Use Video Stories To:

✦ Document an event, action, or phenomenon, like reactions in a science experiment.

✦ Document and analyze technique, such as solving equations, determining narrative structure of paragraphs, poetry, or essays, or studying the skills of a sport.

✦ Record a time-lapse of a creation process that takes a long time, such as painting a mural, building a robot, or the growth of a plant.

## What Video Brings to Storytelling

**Movement as visual evidence.** Think of the ways video can show how an animal moves or feeds, the way a soccer player "bends" a ball to make a goal, or the flight path of a rocket—the movement made possible with video helps us understand the concepts of these kinds of phenomena more accurately.

**Movement as context.** Video allows the viewer to see changes over time and how people interact with one another. Moving the camera during recording can reveal spatial relationships.

**Time remapping.** Slowing down or speeding up video can help us get a more accurate understanding of phenomena, sometimes revealing new information that would be impossible to discern using any other medium. This is helpful in science and also in performance-based curriculum like art or athletics, when analyzing body movement.

**Image and sound in sync.** Some phenomena can only be truly understood with the combination of image and sound, such as a recording of a thunderstorm or testimony of a documentary interview.

## Data Visualization: Painting by Numbers

It's difficult to make sense of raw numbers by staring at a spreadsheet or reading descriptions in paragraphs of text. The best way to make sense of numerical data is often to picture it. That's where data visualizations come in. Pictorial representations of numbers, like charts and graphs, literally help us connect the dots to make sense of data and clearly explain to an audience what they mean.

# What Data Visualization Brings to Storytelling

**Understand relationships.** Bar graphs, scattergrams, and vector maps show how data compare to one another and help reveal similarities and differences.

**Reveal patterns.** Pictorial representation of data helps us see trends and changes over time, like global temperatures in the past 200 years, or the number of women in the workplace since the 1950s.

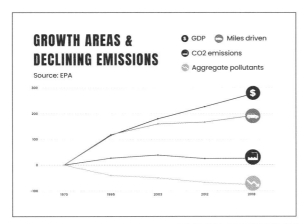

*FIGURE 2.3  Pictorial representation provides more clarity and understanding than raw numbers.*

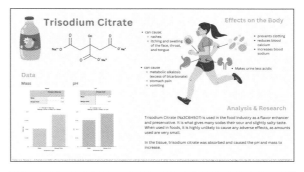

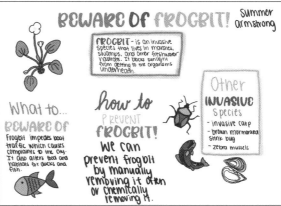

*FIGURE 2.4  Infographics combine images, text, and data to communicate ideas clearly to an audience. Images created by Saipragnya Akula (top) and Summer Armstrong (bottom).*

## Data Visualizations for the Rest of Us

Charts and graphs aren't just for math and science students. There are many kinds of data whose story we can visually represent—and therefore understand better—in every subject area. These might include:

✦ using timelines to sequentially view historical moments, evolutionary or geological events, or show a sequence of steps in a process

✦ creating tables to make comparisons and organize information like data about different planets or how to conjugate verbs of foreign languages

✦ designing graphs that compare demographic information about important figures related to your curricular area, like the age, gender, or race of often-referenced scientists, authors, or musicians, and compare that to your community or state population

✦ taking the temperature of your community by polling students' and community members' reactions to content in your curriculum, like pieces of literature, historical events, class projects, or future areas of study

*Find out more about tools to create data visualizations in appendix A.*

# Illustrations: Pictorial Representations

If you've ever tried to explain to someone how to carve a turkey over the phone or made someone upset when your ironic text didn't land the way you intended, you quickly realized the limits of words.

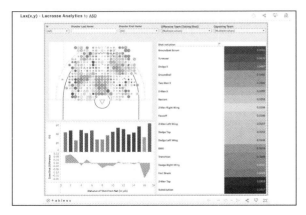

**FIGURE 2.5** *Images like this heat map of shots taken on goal for lacrosse can bridge math, sports, and student interests. Courtesy Jesse McNulty.*

**FIGURE 2.6** **Symbolic:** *Convey important information quickly without the need for words.*

Illustrations are a great way to help students and audiences make sense of a topic by showing relationships, organizing content, and conveying non-verbal information, especially when a technique or process is too complex for words, or when the audience might have difficulty reading or understanding text (Bobek & Tversky, 2016). They can include everything from furniture assembly instructions to book covers to memes.

# What Illustrations Bring to Storytelling

**Clarity and simplicity.** Sometimes it's best to "just show me!" Universal symbols for things like stop signs, electrical hazards, or nuclear radiation are needed when safety is too important to be left to interpretation.

**Accessibility.** Words may prevent younger learners, language learners, or those with learning disabilities from understanding concepts.

**Emotional and interpretive connection.** Book, album, and podcast cover art can get attention and create an emotional relationship toward a work. Students can create illustrations to show their interpretation of a story and help the audience see a story in new ways.

**Nonverbal cues like irony or humor.** Editorial cartoons and memes use satire to activate high-level thinking skills in the author and audience. These types of projects add another level of interpretation to subject matter that can help us see stories through the lens of pop culture, and the relation of our curriculum to current events.

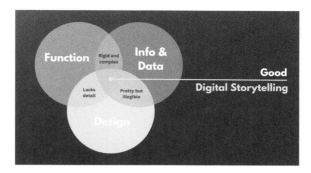

**FIGURE 2.7** *Diagrams like these help provide clarity by showing relationships and context.*

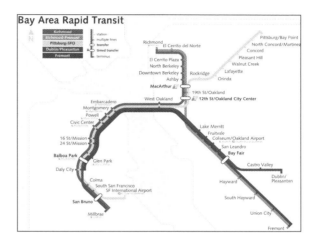

**FIGURE 2.8** *Use maps to sort information spatially and show relationships between information.*

## Diagrams

Everyone who's assembled furniture from IKEA knows how helpful images can be when understanding a complex process, and when words alone don't make sense. Diagrams can also help us show relationships and provide a way to organize information, like Venn diagrams and company organizational charts.

In the same way we rely on sentence diagrams or the periodic table to organize and bring visual clarity to our curriculum, use diagrams in student stories to help them explain relationships and context.

## Maps and Charts

Maps are for much more than seeing countries, topography, or roads. According to Carissa Carter of Stanford d.school in her book *The Secret Language of Maps*, a map can be defined as "information that is sorted spatially and depicted visually" (p. 15). Create maps for projects like family trees, timelines, treasure maps, and star charts.

## Editorial Illustrations

If you've stopped in your tracks to pick up a book in a store, paused your scrolling through social media to read an online article, listened to a podcast for the first time, or bought new music, it was probably because of an eye-catching illustration. Editorial illustrations are artwork created to visualize and reflect the concepts of another medium, like a book, music album, or magazine article, and are frequently used as part of marketing strategies.

Editorial illustrations are one of my favorite storytelling projects because they require deep, critical thinking where students translate abstract concepts into visual representations. In this process, they draw on their knowledge of design and color theory, metaphor, and symbolism, and make cultural and historical references. Language arts teachers may already have a book cover assignment in their curriculum, and editorial illustrations are also a great way to help students conceptualize abstract ideas in science, math, and social studies.

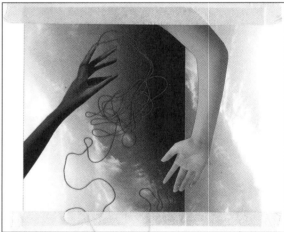

**FIGURE 2.9** *Use illustrations to create cover art for books, albums, or podcasts. This is the cover art for a student podcast about the experiences of BIPOC students at my school (top) and the editorial illustration created by my student Natalee Park for the same podcast (bottom). See projects for illustration in chapter 13.*

# Know What I Meme?

Sometimes, explaining yourself or a cultural moment requires a sense of humor, irony, or even sarcasm. A social media phenomenon that has emerged in the past few years is the meme: an image, usually a photo taken from news or other websites, with text added to create a social or political commentary. Social scientists and politicos have begun to pay close attention to memes as a powerful way to create perceptions (or misperceptions) about a person, group of people, or political topic, especially in these times when audiences have short attention spans and often create meaning from headlines or social media posts. Student-created memes are a great way to activate critical thinking about a topic in a way that is powerful and relevant.

*Find out how to use image-based storytelling in your classroom in chapter 13.*

**FIGURE 2.10** *Memes combine images and text to make a social or political commentary. This image, created by my student Vanessa Lopez, was inspired by artist Barbara Kruger.*

15

CHAPTER 2

Beyond Words: The Power of Multimedia Storytelling

# CHAPTER 3
# FINDING THE BEST WAYS TO TELL A STORY

Flashy videos and cool graphics are fun to make, but they should always be created in the service of conveying information clearly to other people. Even if you've mastered videography or crafting a beautiful data visualization, it won't mean anything unless you can use these tools to find and attract an audience and effectively explain ideas to busy people who may not initially be interested in what you have to say.

In this chapter, we explore the secrets of how to tell effective stories by determining your goals, finding the best medium for your story, and learning how to market your project.

## Choosing the Best Medium

It can be tempting to choose a storytelling medium because of its novelty or because it seems like a creative challenge. Effective stories can come from experimentation like this, but the learning experience might fall short if the content and student learning outcomes aren't the priority. There are many factors that help put choices about storytelling medium into context.

## Questions to Ask When Choosing a Storytelling Medium

Before you begin creating a storytelling project, consider your goals, resources, and student ability.

✦ What are your learning outcomes for the project? What do you want students to learn or express through their stories? Is it to become proficient with certain skills like using the Pythagorean theorem to measure buildings, hone public speaking skills to interview experts, or learn to analyze data to create an infographic? What are the best ways to express that knowledge or demonstrate those skills?

* What tools do you have access to? Some laptops don't have cameras, microphones, or touch screens for drawing, which could make video, audio, photography, and illustration projects difficult. What software do your students have access to? Is it free or is there a license fee?

* How experienced are your students? Have they made digital stories before? If they have, you can build on prior experience to make more complex projects.

* How does emotional and intellectual development impact the complexity of stories? Kindergarteners are very capable of making videos, but even high school seniors can struggle when working on complex projects like documentaries. Scaffold assignments to strengthen storytelling skills and respect the limits of complexity and attention span.

* How much time do you have? Some storytelling projects, like photo markups or a self-reflection audio recording, can be completed in just a

| MEDIUM | EASY STORY | COMPLEX STORY |
|---|---|---|
| Photography | A single photo documenting a historical place or a scientific phenomenon in your community | A digital book anthology of photo essays that combine text, audio, and multiple photographs |
| Time to complete | A few minutes or more | Several days to several weeks |
| Audio | Recording of a self-reflection or interview with one other person | A podcast episode or series that includes scripts, music, sound effects, and a series logo design |
| Time to complete | A few minutes | Several days to several weeks or more |
| Data Visualization | A pie chart depicting percentages of materials that comprise a material sample (e.g., rocks, metals, seawater, etc.) | A chart comparing literary genres by country and date |
| Time to complete | A few minutes to an hour | An hour or more |
| Video | A slow-motion video recording to analyze movement (e.g., athlete or dancer performance, a model rocket launch, etc.) | A documentary or video news story |
| Time to complete | A few minutes plus time to analyze | A few hours to several weeks or more |

*FIGURE 3.1 How long do multimedia stories take to complete?* It depends. Here's a comparison chart to help gauge what you might expect.

few minutes. Others, like documentaries, might take weeks or months of planning, recording, and editing.

## Honor the Content

While it might be important to use a specific medium to build skills (learning data analysis by making an infographic, for example, or learning interview skills by creating a podcast), our ultimate choice of storytelling media should be based on the content itself—some ideas just come across more clearly in one medium than in others. Social media, for example, is best for images and video, while podcasts can only provide audio. Digital books can contain all media, while video has a weakness when it comes to text. Photographs are relatively

easy to make and send information quickly to an audience. Others, like a podcast series or video documentary, take more time to create but have space to convey complex concepts.

## Multi-multimedia Stories

Sometimes, a single medium doesn't do justice to an idea or concept, and stories often need to be told using a constellation of media to paint the clearest picture for an audience. An infographic, for example, can be enhanced with text that explains the chart and provides context or background information. A video documentary might be strengthened by embedding historical photos, data visualizations, or maps.

| CONTENT TYPE | MEDIUM | EXAMPLE |
| --- | --- | --- |
| Data | Data visualization | Graphs and charts |
| Context | Illustrations, infographics | Charts, timelines, and maps |
| Movement | Video, animation | Recordings of phenomena, slow motion video |
| Change | Infographics, photography, video | Charts, photo essays, time-lapse or slow-motion video |
| Empathy and Emotion | Audio, video, photography | Podcasts, interviews, portraits |
| Documentation/Visual Evidence | Photography, video | Photojournalism, documentaries, journalism |
| Commentary/Analysis/Expository Expression | Illustrations, audio, video | Editorial illustrations, commentaries or opinion stories as podcasts or videos, explainer videos |

*FIGURE 3.2  The medium is the message:* How to choose the best format for your content..

## The Free Spirits

by Natalee Park

Society rarely encourages originality, yet high school takes it to another level. This seems to apply especially to Mira Costa, where kids are expected to kill what makes each of them unique. I've noticed in my time here that it not only comes from peer pressure, but also from the expectations of teachers and adults we are expected to seek guidance from. Yet, these three girls have found a way to rebel against the mainstream. I hope to give them justice through my photographs, portraying the independent and unconcerned disposition they embody. I've had them in my art classes for nearly 4 years. Even through all the pressure brought by middle and high school, they still choose to dress, act, and even sit in any way that they want.

Listen to my interview with Sarah that I recorded in October of 2019.

Photographs by Natalee Park

Listen to the photographer's reactions as they completed this assignment

*FIGURE 3.3 Stories like this digital book can combine multiple media to convey a variety of information. This page content was created by my student, Natalee Park.*

Anthology stories like digital books and websites can place different media side by side to enhance understanding of a concept. Consider a digital book like the one above that has a gallery of photographs, a paragraph of text, and audio clips that share the voices of people involved in the story.

# How to Create an Engaging Story

It's not enough for authors to be passionate about stories we create—we have to help our audiences feel this passion, too, and that means making their experience as enjoyable and easy to access as possible.

## Captivate: How to Get and Hold Audience Attention

Advertisers, marketing experts, and social media influencers know that the most important part of a story is getting the attention of your audience in the first place. This also applies to student stories, which are often created for busy, distracted audiences beyond the classroom. Paying attention to the hook of a story—the ways we can grab and hold an audience's attention—not only helps our students find a wider audience for their stories but also creates awareness of their own viewing habits and the ways advertisers and others might manipulate them to get their attention, too.

# Advertising for Good

Advertising techniques that convince an audience to buy a product often play on the psychological, social, and emotional needs of an audience. While this can often get a bad rap if the advertisement promotes consumerism or encourages unhealthy products or behaviors, the same techniques can be used for social good. When scientists need to share important information about health care issues or the environment, or a community is trying to encourage positive behaviors like anti-racism or anti-bullying, it's vital that these stories use the same techniques as advertisers to convince an audience to "buy" positive behaviors and mindsets.

*Learn more about advertising for good in the PSA project in chapter 14.*

There are several ways a story can get and hold an audience's attention. One of the best ways is teasing the audience by hinting at what they can expect in your story. Here are some ways to do this.

✦ **Raise a question.** Doing so addresses an existing question the audience has (or didn't know they had before you asked it) and creates the need to find out the answer.

✦ **Use catchy and creative titles, headlines, or captions.** Draw on student creative writing skills and use literary devices like irony, humor, and hyperbole to create surprising titles.

✦ **Provide a novel image, sound, or situation.** These literally eye-catching elements act as visual questions and narrative riddles that beg to be solved.

✦ **Offer a solution to a problem faced by the audience.** Using feedback from empathy interviews, write headlines that connect your story to audience needs. (See chapter 6 for more about empathy interviews.)

✦ **Start with the familiar.** Audiences often connect with stories better when they recognize themselves or someone they know in a story, or when we use examples from life that they are familiar with.

✦ **Use story structures to create mystery and suspense.** Long projects like podcasts or video stories can tease the audience with prologues and cliffhanger openings similar to many TV shows. Try using the *in medias res* story structure, where we begin a story near the end of the plot line, then circle back to find out how we got there.

✦ **Create stories as mysteries to be solved or adventures to follow.** Even if students don't find a definitive answer to their question (there may not be one yet), the excitement and fun of a story lies in the journey, engaging audiences as they come along with the storyteller through their process of discovery.

## Find Eyeballs: Take Your Story to Your Audience

Your students aren't famous authors yet, so we can't assume people will knock down doors to find their projects. Put student stories in front of your audience where they are, rather than asking them to find you. Find out where different audiences consume content. On websites? Social media channels? Email or word of mouth? Share and market projects on platforms where your audience is already likely to be, which can often be based on demographics like age, gender, or region. Older adults may not be savvy with social media the way middle and high school students are, for example, and elementary students may not have access to those channels at all.

## Make the Story Accessible

Well-crafted stories should be easy to understand and shouldn't ask the audience to work hard. Making stories accessible for people of all abilities is a great opportunity for your students to reach the widest audience possible, increase story clarity, and build empathy for the needs of others. Everyone can benefit from content that is designed for accessibility by:

✦ reducing eye strain

✦ increasing fluency

✦ improving comprehension

✦ allowing the audience to consume content in a variety of conditions (like understanding videos by reading closed captions in noisy locations or where sound might disturb others)

| ORIGINAL | NEW VERSION | WHY THIS WORKS BETTER |
|---|---|---|
| "Report finds new evidence about how to study better" | "Ace tests and raise your grades with these study techniques verified by scientists" | Address audience needs and concerns with specifics from the research study |
| "The school reveals plans for a new library building with updated features" | "Plans for a 50,000-square-foot library puts community, digital life first" | Specific details make the accompanying story enticing |

**FIGURE 3.4 Capture attention with captions:** *Catchy headlines and clever captions can help get the audience's attention. In the era of social media, titles and short summaries may be the only information your audience ever gets from a story since they may not take time to experience your stories in their entirety.*

# How to Make Stories Accessible

**Closed Captions.** Closed captions on video stories help audiences understand dialogue and voiceover without the use of sound. This increases comprehension for those with auditory processing issues, or when conditions don't allow sound to be on—like noisy classrooms. It's also a great way to aid in learning new languages.

**Alt Text.** Alt text is a brief description added to images and photographs that can be read aloud by digital devices to help audiences with visual impairments.

**Design.** Using simple, high-contrast design techniques for digital books, social media posts, and websites can reduce eye strain and increase fluency. Avoid cluttered layouts, busy backgrounds, garish colors, and hard-to-read fonts. Use appropriate line spacing for text.

*See more resources about accessibility in appendix C.*

# Marketing Your Story and Storytellers

A story isn't finished until it finds an audience. Help stories get past the noise of our busy world by creating a marketing plan to share student stories and provide transparency about how they were created. Even the marketing itself is a type of storytelling! Here are some suggestions for marketing student stories:

✦ Publish links to student stories in school email newsletters and websites.

✦ Create eye-catching social media graphic cards using a free online graphics tool.

✦ Share the student storytelling process with still photos, screenshots, or time-lapse videos made while the students work. Share these on social media, emails, and class websites throughout the project process (if working on longer assignments) or once the stories are complete.

✦ Share the final project (or hyperlinks) with experts and others who contributed to the story, along with a thank-you note.

✦ Leverage word of mouth. Talk with parents, colleagues, and administration, or have students present their work at schoolwide events.

✦ Always make clear the value and importance of your stories by answering this question for the audience: "Why should I care?"

# CHAPTER 4
# ELEMENTS OF A GOOD STORY

*Every story has a beginning, middle, and end, but not necessarily in that order.*

**—Jean-Luc Godard**

For years, I only had a gut feeling if a story was good or bad or mediocre, but I never really knew the secrets of how authors and directors made stories magical. In this chapter, I pull back the curtain on how to make stories clearer and more engaging, leaving the audience wanting more.

## Clarity and Purpose
### Know Your Goals as an Author

If an author isn't clear about what their story is and why they're telling it, their audience won't be either. Having narrow, specific goals for the project makes it easier to create the story and results in a more effective final product.

✦ Use the story pitch process discussed in chapter 5 and develop a focus statement to guide research and the entire storytelling process. Stick with your plan!

✦ Select one or two main ideas that are the most important to communicate through this story. If the audience forgets everything else, what should they remember?

## Less is More: The Importance of Brevity

In the same way movies struggle to represent the entirety of novels, multimedia digital stories are different from essays or reports: they can't cover the same density of information. Audiences also consume multimedia stories differently from text-only stories, and student authors need to respect the viewing habits of their end user if they want to be successful. All of this means that we need to adjust our expectations of the scope of what multimedia stories can cover and create stories that embrace their strengths instead.

**FIGURE 4.1** *Design social media graphics to appeal to specific audiences. The image on the left uses illustrations, fonts, and colors that appeal to students. The image on the right—with cleaner fonts, composition, and an image of students—reflects a professionalism that resonates with adults.*

When students need to address long, complex topics with multimedia stories, consider these techniques:

+ Serialize large topics into multiple bite-sized stories. These can be created sequentially over time, or student teams can each take on a different aspect of a larger topic.

+ Use hyperlinks to provide further context, resources, or citations.

## Design for Your End User

We each have unique life experiences, and our favorite movie, music, and clothing preferences, but what works for us may be incomprehensible or hideous for others. The same is true of the stories we create, and it's important to understand how to make content and aesthetic choices that make our stories effective for our audience, not just ourselves or our friends.

+ Have students role-play or even interview members of an audience to determine what they already know or wonder about a story topic.

+ Understand their audience's existing story consumption habits (such as where they get their news, and what kinds of story formats they prefer).

## Familiarity: Context and Points of Reference

Comparing new information to something the audience already understands or is familiar with makes the story relatable and helps with comprehension. This can be done through writing voice-over scripts or visually when creating illustrations and data visualizations. Make comparisons that might use anecdotes, historical context, analogies, or comparable measurements. A blue whale may be as long as a soccer field, for example, and a snail may be the size of your thumb.

## Knowledge vs. Entertainment

Stories should be fun and exciting, not boring or tedious, especially for the non-captive audiences that our students are designing for. Use storytelling techniques that keep the audience engaged so that they won't miss out on important content, and students will have a greater chance of creating a meaningful impact. Surprise and delight audiences with these techniques:

✦ **Writing style.** Voiceover scripts should use conversational language and be performed with enthusiasm. Captions and titles should be clever and surprising.

✦ **Find captivating characters.** In stories with interviews, try to choose people who are dynamic and charismatic, or have a compelling story to tell.

✦ **Create dynamic images.** Whether it's photography or video, encourage the use of dynamic, surprising compositions. Infographics should be colorful.

✦ **Style and design.** Use contemporary design choices for fonts, colors, and composition. Many free online design tools have templates to get you started.

✦ **Use music.** Music can create a fun mood and enhance style. There are now many choices for royalty-free music for videos and social media posts.

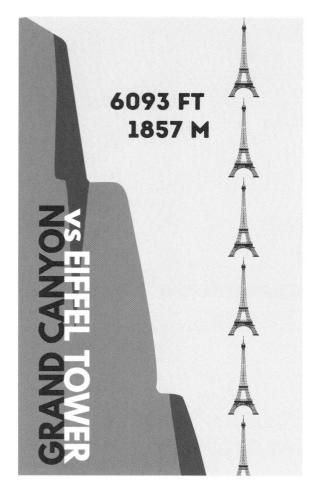

**FIGURE 4.2** *Providing examples and referencing commonly understood concepts helps put new information or ideas in perspective and show their significance.*

✦ **Use dynamic editing.** Just as a speaker can drone on and become boring, so can videos and podcasts if they're not tight, crisp, and edited with a varied rhythm. Photographic series can also benefit from surprising sequencing.

*Look at appendix A for tools and resources for creating good design and effective multimedia stories.*

**FIGURE 4.3** *Design can help us relate to content, provide clarity (including accessibility), and create a personality for a topic or event. In the same way correct grammar and concise writing provide clarity and a professionally dressed speaker garners respect, so, too do well-designed graphics help us develop a strong relationship to content. The image on the left is busy, uses too many fonts, and has low contrast between text and background images, making it difficult to read. The image on the right uses sans serif fonts, clear contrast, and groups content to organize information.*

# Structure: Stories as Learning Quests

The thrill and excitement of stories always comes from wondering about the outcome. Our students embark on a journey of discovery—a quest—as they learn through the creation of digital stories, and the audience learns in a similar way when they embark on an adventure designed by the author.

Unlike traditional reports and essays, truly engaging stories are based on surprise. Begin stories with questions and wonder, and then structure them around the discovery process. Create exciting stories by embracing techniques like suspense and mystery, and story genres like quests. Create mystery or suspense with *in medias res* story structures and flashbacks. Avoid giving away the most important info at the beginning of your story!

# Elements of Story

There are three main elements of stories, and all stories—fiction or nonfiction—rely on these elements to be successful.

## Theme/Focus Statement

Themes are big ideas or questions the author wants the audience to think about and that help guide the author as she makes choices about story content and style. Focus statements are questions that a story strives to answer, such as "What is our role in habitat destruction?" or "How can we identify reliable sources of information?"

## Character

A person or entity that we follow through the journey of a story is a character. In nonfiction stories, characters can show up as individuals, groups of people, animal species, ecosystems, or other entities that are affected by a topic.

## Conflict

Conflict is a series of obstacles that characters struggle to overcome in order to achieve their goals. Depending on the subject matter, stories might have conflicts such as gentrification making it too expensive for a historic population to remain in their homes; climate change affecting a particular animal's food chain; or the systemic challenges immigrants face when trying to move to a new country. Or, if the student authors are the characters of a story, the conflict could be their search to solve a problem.

| | ELA | SCIENCE | SOCIAL STUDIES |
|---|---|---|---|
| TOPIC | Comparing literary genres | Measuring the salinity of an estuary | Immigration |
| THEME/FOCUS STATEMENT | How do economic trends affect the publishing and readership of different genres? | What are ways that estuaries self-regulate water quality? | How are culinary traditions influenced by other cultures and countries? |
| CHARACTER | Genre (concept) | The estuary (habitat) | Immigrants (people) |
| CONFLICT | Economic trends, technology | Humans, industry, weather | Economic trends, immigration law, industry, global conflicts, agriculture |

FIGURE 4.4 **The story of learning:** Use the elements of story to create an engaging experience for the audience.

# Why the End Is the Most Important Part of a Story

Storytelling is much more than listing statistics and reciting formulas—it's about connecting the dots to help the audience understand what all these facts mean. We do this in stories by providing context and understanding the significance of a topic when applied in the real world. Perhaps the most important role of student storytellers is to help the audience develop an accurate, faithful relationship to information. It's helpful here to include supporting exercises in logic and reasoning and concepts such as the difference between correlation and causation.

## Misinterpreting information: Confirmation Bias

When we leave the meaning of a story completely up to the audience, either by presenting just raw data, statements, or facts or by failing to provide context, they can have wildly different interpretations of information, leading to an inaccurate understanding of the topic. As audience members, we interpret the meaning of facts based on our life experience and who we are: age, culture, prior knowledge, or sociopolitical lens. Misinterpretation of facts is also an effect of confirmation bias, where we seek facts and ideas that confirm what we already believe, and disregard or discount those that conflict with our beliefs.

It's important for students to pay special attention to the end of their stories and how they draw conclusions about their topic. This helps ensure that their message is accurately received and is faithful to the facts. It also creates an awareness of their own biases and helps them identify areas for further study.

## What Now? Where Do We Go from Here?

After context and analogies, one of the best ways to help the audience make sense of a topic is to help them see what the future holds for the story topic and how they might use this information in their own lives. For student authors, this is an important exercise in extrapolation, inference, and how to see actions and events not as isolated incidents, but as part of a wider context.

Help students draw accurate conclusions in their stories by asking themselves:

✦ What does this all mean?

✦ What impact does this have on _____?

✦ What do experts say can be done about it?

✦ Who haven't we heard from yet?

✦ What new questions do you have about this topic, and what do you wonder about now?

Good conclusions include answers to questions like these:

✦ When will an element in this story happen/be done/go into effect?

✦ What are leaders or experts doing—or failing to do—to solve this problem?

*FIGURE 4.5* *Our psychological disposition often leads us to find information that we already agree with. When presented with raw facts or simple definitions, the audience will often view those facts through their own lens and may come to incorrect conclusions about what data or facts actually mean.*

✦ How can the audience use this new information (to inform good decisions)?

✦ What are some actions the audience can take with this information? (How can the audience participate in/do something about this topic?)

✦ What are some topics for future study?

This is a powerful learning model because it asks students to make sense of all their research, see this story project as one moment in a continuum of learning, and understand that there's still more to know.

# CHAPTER 5

# HOW TO CREATE A STORY, STEP BY STEP

In this chapter, we roll up our sleeves and talk about the practical steps of how to create and publish stories. Use this chapter as a road map for creating the storytelling projects in part III and as a logistical guide as you create story lessons and lead students through the process.

## 10 Steps of the Storytelling Process

Like the design thinking process we will discuss in chapter 8, think of each of these steps as a mini workshop, where students have time to brainstorm, get feedback, test their ideas, and make adjustments before moving to the next step. I've found that even a few minutes of workshopping helps students elevate their ideas, avoid problems in future steps of the process, and have a stronger final product.

### 1. Research

Use traditional research methods and qualitative techniques like empathy interviews to help students learn about a topic and discover facts that may develop into their story. Have students identify facts and concepts from their research that resonated with them or stood out in some way—these may become the basis for their story or be important to share with their audience.

### 2. Ideation and Brainstorming

Based on their research, students develop ideas for what their story might become. Sometimes the wildest ideas are the stories most worth telling, so encourage students to avoid self-censoring or evaluating before they've put every idea on the table. *Find out more about how to come up with good ideas in chapter 6.*

Compile a list of potential story ideas, then hone the options down based on criteria that you and your students develop, such as timeliness, originality, significance, impact on the audience, relevance

# Sample Story Pitches

Story pitches are concise, specific, and help students find clarity in what their project is about.

## Story Pitch 1

To make new students to our school feel welcome, we propose creating a "Who's Who" digital book with new student portraits and an audio recording of them sharing what excites them most about being at our school. This matters because it's always hard to be new and make new friends, and the book is a great way for teachers and other students to learn about people they might not see every day.

## Story Pitch 2

With all the traffic before and after school, we want to find out how many students walk, bike, or use alternative forms of transportation. This story will be a set of data visualizations created from a poll of students and teachers about their transportation habits and perceptions. These graphs and charts will be shared on our class Instagram account. We believe this hard data can help the school make the best decisions about traffic mitigation, parking, and safety.

to the assignment topic, etc. This is where students begin to develop potential focus statements.

To keep students focused and accountable, have them write down the purpose for a story by asking themselves:

+ What is my story really about (beyond the surface, initial inspiration)?
+ Why am I telling this story (what stories am I potentially leaving out)?
+ What do I want the audience to understand or be able to do once they've experienced my story?
+ What information, examples, evidence, and explanation will I need to help the audience understand the concepts in my story?

## 3. The Pitch

Adapted from pitches that screenwriters and entrepreneurs make when seeking funding for their projects, a story pitch is a written or oral proposal for a story project that includes the topic and initial ideas for content, format, and style. The idea is to get students to provide clarity for themselves about their story's purpose and form and to elicit feedback to refine their ideas before starting the project. It's worthwhile to make time for even a brief in-class story pitch workshop, but if your time is limited, at least have students write down their concept.

A good story pitch should:

+ Be concise (only two or three sentences) and specifically describe content they might include.

✦ Include an idea for the story focus statement (the driving question this story strives to answer). *Learn more about focus statements in chapter 8.*

✦ Explain why this story is important and why it's worthy of making and sharing with others. Answer the question, "Why does this matter?"

## 4. Story Mapping

Like mind maps for other projects, story maps help students see the entire project at once to help them plan and pace their work. It also helps them see relationships between sections of a story (like a timeline or schematic), and what content they may need to create (shot lists, interviews to record). This is especially important for complex projects like podcasts, explainer videos, and documentaries, but can be helpful for simpler projects, too, especially for beginning students who are not yet familiar with the storytelling process. Story mapping can take many forms: outlines, whiteboard drawings, storyboards, and flowcharts.

Idea maps might include:

✦ page outlines for a digital book

✦ episode topics and summaries for a podcast series

✦ a publication calendar for social media posts

✦ website site maps

## 5. Writing

Write outlines, develop interview questions, and begin writing voiceover scripts for explainer videos, podcasts, and documentaries. Stories with text (digital books, social posts, etc.) need a draft of the content. *See chapter 15 for script formats and guidance about writing for digital stories.*

## 6. Pre-Production Planning

Prepare to produce the story by addressing these logistics.

✦ Schedule interviews with experts or stakeholders.

✦ From the story maps developed earlier, make lists of media to acquire, such as shot lists of video or audio footage to record, photographs to take, graphics to create, etc.

✦ Determine what equipment might be needed to complete the project, such as cameras, tripods, green screens, microphones, video conferencing apps, etc.

## 7. Production

Record, collect, or create media outlined in the pre-production phase. Review this content for quality and accuracy, and re-record if it's not up to snuff.

## 8. Editing

Like the curator of a museum or editor of a book, students in this phase select the best and most relevant media, refining and organizing what was created in the production phase. It's common to veer from the original outline and reorganize information based on new insights and reactions to what students have discovered in the production process.

✦ Edit audio or video footage.

✦ Select and arrange images in a photography series.

✦ Create captions and titles for illustrations.

# How Long Does It Take to Produce a Story?

Estimates for how long it takes to create story projects can be found in part III, but timeframes for completing story projects depend on many factors such as:

+ **Complexity of the medium.** Video takes longer than photography, for example.

+ **Expectations of quality.** Allowing time for pre-planning and revision lengthens the timing.

+ **Student experience.** The more familiar students are with the process and tools, the faster they can create.

## 9. Final Assembly

Polish and put the final touches on the story, such as designing the layout of a digital book or slide deck, or adding titles and music to a video or podcast. Make final checks for accuracy and technical precision.

## 10. Publishing and Marketing

Share stories with your audience by posting videos or podcasts to streaming services, publishing a digital book, or posting photos and illustrations to a website or social media channel. Promote the project on social media, in school newsletters, and through word of mouth so that others can find your stories.

# Learning Together: Why, When, and How to Form Teams

Digital storytelling projects help students build relationships not only to the content but also to each other. Working in teams helps students develop skills and build their capacity to work productively within a group. When The World Economic Forum polls employers every five years, collaboration is consistently at the top of the most in-demand job skills for future workers (Whiting, 2020). Learning to work alongside others to achieve a common goal also provides opportunities for students to develop social skills like leadership, problem-solving, and conflict management.

Here are some advantages of team projects:

+ **Divide labor.** A big topic or complex project isn't as daunting when multiple students are sharing the workload.

+ **Share expertise.** When students join forces, they each bring their unique talents that make a project stronger than if it was completed individually. Some students are better at public speaking, writing, or photography, for example. These skills also tend to rub off on other students, as they organically learn from peers who mentor each other and share insights in an informal way.

✦ **Increase innovation.** Research shows that when people from diverse backgrounds work together, they are more innovative and creative (Lu , Murnighan & Connelly, 2017). For this reason, consider creating teams that are less homogeneous, despite the urge to pair up students who are already friends or who get along.

✦ **Create belonging.** When everyone has a job to do and works toward a common goal, it can build a sense of shared purpose.

✦ **Share equipment.** If you don't have a 1:1 classroom, team projects may be your only choice.

Digital story projects allow flexibility when making decisions about individual assignments vs. group projects. It's not always an either/or choice.

## What Makes a Good Teammate?

Before you begin group projects, work with students to develop a class culture and set of shared values about inclusiveness and expectations about

what it means to be a good teammate (Wise, 2021). One of the biggest conflicts in school and work is when we have different expectations of quality, work ethic, and communication. To develop shared expectations, lead students through a discussion of questions like these, then post a list of their agreed-upon responses in your classroom:

✦ What are the traits of a good teammate?

✦ What do you want others to know about how you prefer to work?

✦ What does it mean to be "professional"?

✦ What's the difference between "having fun" and being proud of your work?

## Tips for a Fun and Productive Storytelling Process

Creating stories is fun and exciting, but even the most experienced authors can get tangled up in the many moving parts of producing a story if

| INDIVIDUAL ASSIGNMENT | TEAM PROJECT EQUIVALENT |
|---|---|
| Collecting evidence of foliage diversity through photography | A digital book or website anthology of photos captured by multiple students while traveling on winter break or gathered from their own neighborhoods |
| Audio recording of an interview with an expert | A podcast where each member of a production team is responsible for producing one episode of a series, on a theme and topic agreed upon by the group |
| Audio recording of a poem with an accompanying editorial illustration | A literary magazine (digital book) where students organize into a leadership structure and elicit contributions from many students beyond their own classroom |

*FIGURE 5.1 To team or not to team:* A comparison of individual assignments and a team project equivalent.

# Is Collaboration Cheating?

Schools sometimes discourage collaborative projects in which students develop and share ideas together because it can be hard to discern the work of individual students when assigning grades. Just as sports teams benefit from players who have many assists and improve the chemistry of the team, letting students work together can elevate the quality of everyone's learning.

For those times when individual grades are required, provide students with specific roles, such as graphic designer or writer, and assess them on that work. Or provide steps in the process that are completed individually, such as developing their own research and story pitch, then have students collaborate when creating the story. I like to use narrative self-evaluations at the end of a project, where students can reflect on their contributions and those of their teammates. Students are usually eager to provide details, and the process activates metacognitive thinking about their learning.

*Find out more about assessment in chapter 9.*

they're not careful. Having a workflow that keeps projects on track and elevates the best ideas is essential to facilitating a productive and enjoyable learning experience.

## Keep It Short and Start with the Basics

While it's admirable to be ambitious, it's always best to start small, especially when students are new to digital storytelling.

+ Create short projects to avoid becoming overwhelmed. One to three photos for a photography story, or 30- or 60-second explainer videos and documentaries, for example.

+ Begin with projects that hone foundational skills, like photography (which is the basis of videography) or audio interviews before moving to podcasts or video documentaries.

## Design Sprint: Pace Learners with Deadlines

Procrastination will always get the best of us, and offering a single deadline for a story project is a recipe for disaster, especially for complex projects like videos, podcasts, and books. But even the simplest of digital stories can benefit from multiple deadlines around these common steps of the storytelling process:

+ ideation

+ revision

+ production

+ publication/marketing

# Feedback as a Gift

Giving and receiving feedback is a tricky thing to do, yet it is one of the most important skills our students can learn. The storytelling process allows us to reframe feedback as constructive dialogue rather than negative criticism.

In my classes, we consider feedback an act of generosity: someone takes the time to review another student's work, puts effort into analyzing it, and then gives suggestions to make the work stronger. Receiving critical, constructive feedback is helpful, too, because students can polish and strengthen their work before it's finally published for everyone to see.

These are some considerations when creating time and space for story workshops:

✦ **Create a safe space.** Discuss and model constructive feedback both online and in person. Work with students to develop and adopt community norms.

✦ **Focus the feedback.** Choose a specific element of the storytelling process to address, such as developing a focus statement or reviewing a draft of a script.

✦ **Review work in advance.** Have students post drafts of their projects on your class LMS and have them look at each other's work before they come to class. This makes face-to-face class time more productive.

How much time you allot to complete each of these tasks depends on a variety of factors, from the complexity of the projects, to the experience of your students, to your expectations of quality.

*Find out more about timelines for specific projects in part III.*

## Storytelling as a Workshop

Whether it's scientific research, designing a new product, or writing a novel, the best ideas evolve from dialogue between creators, their audience, mentors, and trusted peers. Story workshops give authors opportunities to get feedback from thought partners in order to:

✦ choose the best story topics and focus

✦ check the effectiveness of a story

✦ identify weaknesses in the story and suggestions for improvement

✦ find solutions to storytelling challenges

✦ learn from and be inspired by work being done by others

# CHAPTER 6
# DEVELOPING STORY TOPICS

*Inspiration exists, but it has to find you working.*

—**Pablo Picasso**

One of the most important steps in the storytelling process is the first one: helping students decide which story to tell. This not only affects their engagement throughout the learning process but also asks them to think critically about what they value and to see the importance of paying attention to the world around them.

In this chapter, I share some of my favorite activities for developing story topics and provide advice on how to make choices about which story to tell.

## You Are What You Consume: A Storytelling Audit

Our relationship to story says a lot about who we are and the kinds of stories we choose to tell. What we consider to be a "good" story is often a result of our personality, culture, age, gender, race, experience, and a variety of other traits. There are also subtle, often unrecognized factors that affect which stories we consume and how we evaluate them, such as advertising and social factors like recommendations from friends.

Helping students become aware of the types of stories they currently consume enables them to recognize personal tastes and find biases that might later affect their decisions about which stories they choose to tell and which people and information they include in their projects.

Have students keep track of stories of all kinds that they consume, either actively, like when they choose to watch a YouTube video, or passively, like hearing ads in the background. Then have them respond to these questions:

✦ What kinds of stories do you typically like, or keep coming back to? Which ones do you avoid?

✦ What stories do you have access to? Why?

✦ Who or what is a gatekeeper, controlling the stories you experience? (Parents, schools, etc.?)

✦ What might limit your ability to experience certain stories (language, time zones, age, technology, cost, vision or hearing abilities, neurodivergence, etc.)?

Then have students think about the authors of these stories:

✦ Who created the stories you experience? Describe their demographic traits, such as gender, age, country of origin, race, etc.

✦ What are their motivations for telling you these stories? What's in it for them? What do they want us to do with this information?

✦ What are some potential biases that affect which stories they tell us and what information or perspectives they choose to include?

✦ How do they get their stories to you (social media, word of mouth, etc.) and what are the costs associated with accessing these stories (owning a mobile device, registering for a social media account, paying for a streaming service, watching ads, etc.)?

Have students discuss their reflections and debrief on what they think this might mean for their own knowledge about the world and other people. How do these insights affect how they will create and share their own stories?

# Where Do Good Stories Come From?

Good story topics don't drop out of the sky. They often require an experience or artifact to trigger an emotional or intellectual response that students can eventually develop into a story. There is no one right way to generate story ideas, but the best we can do is give students time to process and reflect on these triggering moments to turn their personal reactions into a powerful engine for learning.

## Teacher- vs. Student-Generated Topics

Honoring self-determination is key to developing students who are independent thinkers, and it helps create a culture of professionalism and respect in the classroom. Inviting students to have a say when making choices about their academic work not only helps them make personal connections to our curriculum, but it also offers opportunities for them to develop high-level critical-thinking skills. And it embraces the concept that there is more than one way to solve a problem.

A data visualization project, for example, might be created around collecting samples as part of a unit about learning scientific research methods. Student choice might mean anything from deciding which phenomenon to collect data about, determining where and how to take samples, figuring out how to choose the most relevant data set to use, and making design decisions about colors and fonts when creating the chart or graph.

Be transparent and share your goals with students so they can understand your decision-making process, including criteria for choosing story topics. Having guidelines keeps projects on track and manageable and can also serve as a creative challenge.

## Topics vs. Themes

Giving assignments typically means asking students to work within a defined space, often called the *topic*. But I find that topics tend to put external limits on how students think about a subject, such as a definition, time period, or genre. Instead, I like to challenge students with *themes*, which are open-ended prompts that tend to spark a more creative way to think about a subject and always lead to a more intriguing result.

While topics can be useful for developing fundamental knowledge and checking for learning, themes invite students to perceive, interpret, or understand a topic in unique ways, thereby activating higher-level thinking and allowing for more flexibility, personalization, and originality.

Open-ended themes allow intellectual flexibility in how students will make decisions about their story projects and also help them grapple with the curriculum in ways that make the most sense for them. These are some themes I've used before and descriptions that help students get started:

+ **In the Shadows.** What is unknown or hiding? Why are people or places marginalized? What is lurking in your heart or mind that is afraid to see the light of day? Where have we not yet traveled to or discovered?

+ **Inside Out.** Is what you seek really there? Expectations turned upside down. What's on the surface and what's beneath?

+ **Not What You'd Expect.** Preconceived ideas. Stereotypes. Decisions that turned out better than you thought they would. People who surprised you (in good ways). What happens when you're wrong?

| TOPIC | THEME |
|-------|-------|
| How rainbows are formed | "Perception" |
| The 14th Amendment to the U.S. Constitution | "Maturity and change" |
| Compare/contrast | "Difference" |

**FIGURE 6.1 Story spark:** *Topics are specific, whereas themes invite a creative interpretation of a concept.*

## Story Generation Techniques

Great ideas don't miraculously appear on demand while sitting in class. They are born from interactions with people, places, and ideas and when we have a mindset that is receptive to new and surprising concepts wherever and whenever they may happen.

### Collecting Ideas: Wonder Journals and Media Logs

My friend and middle school science teacher Leah Lacrosse encourages her students to be curious 24-7 by having them keep Wonder Journals, a collection of ideas, questions, observations, and conversations they continually gather while at school or at home. To enhance creative writing, my cinema students keep dream journals—descriptions of dreams, observations of life, and other creative fragments that appear throughout the day.

Journals can be physical notebooks or digital ones that can capture images, sound, and video. Older students might also collect online articles and resources they encounter by adding them to

**39**

a media log spreadsheet. Any of these ideas could help support a current project or become the seed of inspiration for a future one.

## Idea Safaris

Walking explorations of a particular place, or Idea Safaris, leverage the novelty of seeing something for the first time to spark the imagination and generate ideas for stories. Have students look for details related to your curriculum or story topic, such as sensory details for a poetry unit, sign fonts for a design project, or frequency and repetition for a math assignment. Debrief with students by having them share their findings in small groups or with the entire class. This can help validate students' experiences and help them see the value of unique observations and perspectives of others.

While on safari, students can write or record observations and collect data, such as:

+ light, temperature, materials, languages, sounds
+ emotional reactions/feelings about these places and the people they meet
+ questions that come up as they make their observations

Safaris can be formally structured by providing specific routes or questions for students, or they can be informal routines that students perform regularly. If you don't have the time or budget for a field trip, even regular experiences like the commute to and from school can be an opportunity for an Idea Safari. For example:

+ Take a different route to and from school. What do you notice now that you didn't before?

+ Sit in a different part of the bus/train/car that you take to school. How is your view different? How are the people or places you see different than before?

+ Make a map of your most traveled routes around campus or the places you most often visit. Make it a point to change your route and visit other places at school you haven't been to before.

## Salons and Hackathons

For centuries, artists, politicians, and intellectuals have held salons—intimate gatherings of people where they discuss topical issues. More recently, web and app developers started holding hackathons to generate solutions to bugs or develop new features. Create your own salons by inviting community members to visit classes or by hosting online webinars with authors and experts around the world via video conferencing tools.

## Innovators' Compass

This design thinking tool, developed by former IDEO strategist Ela Ben-Ur, helps students clarify goals and purpose, generate ideas, and make decisions about which ideas to use. This is a great tool for developing story ideas because it centers ideas on the audience (end user), has students reflect on the current state of the community, encourages them to dream big, and provides ways to prioritize ideas based on the question: What matters most? Use it as a flexible framework at any stage of the storytelling process, from generating the main story topic, all the way down to specific choices about design or where and when to publish.

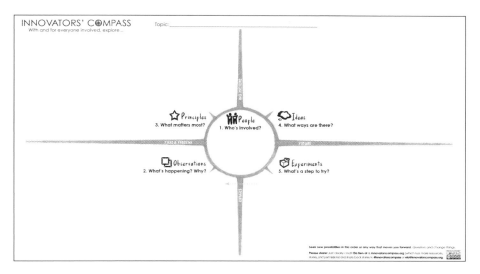

**FIGURE 6.2** *Innovators' Compass is a free tool for generating ideas and solutions, goal setting, and aligning student work to a shared purpose. Find a link to Innovators' Compass in the online Digital Resources.*

## Use Research to Help Students Find Their Passion

Inviting students to create a story based on their research means asking them to pay attention to the world around them and helps them see the value of experts. It also honors their natural sense of curiosity by allowing them to embrace their interests and to evaluate what matters most.

As students conduct research for their projects, have them answer these questions about their findings:

✦ What facts or information surprised you? Why is it so surprising?

✦ What, if anything in your research, challenges what you already knew about this topic?

✦ Out of all your findings, what matters most to you? What might matter most to other people?

✦ How has your thinking about this topic changed now that you have this new information?

## Empathy Interviews

We don't know what we don't know, so ask someone who does. Even scientists, journalists, and businesspeople start from a place of ignorance and need help figuring out what their project should focus on and what information they might need to solve a problem.

A great place to start any story project is with empathy interviews, conversations that students have with someone knowledgeable about a topic so they can get a better sense of its history and context. These are called empathy interviews because they help us understand—or empathize with—stakeholders of a topic. They help students determine what they should research, which experts they might speak with, and potential questions to ask during interviews. They also help reveal students' blind spots so stories can be inclusive, provide context, and be faithful to historical fact.

# Who Is a Stakeholder?

A stakeholder is someone affected by a topic or who otherwise bears some responsibility for the topic. For example, a project about climate justice has stakeholders that might include:

✦ people directly impacted by climate change, such as someone whose life, community, or home has been affected by a wildfire, flood, or drought

✦ politicians and other leaders who are responsible for helping to solve the problem

✦ scientists and other experts who help explain the situation or are finding solutions

Stakeholders may be individuals or organizations such as government agencies, NGOs, school districts, etc.

# Choosing the Best Ideas
## Why This Story and Why Now?

It's tempting for kids—and adults!—to tell stories simply because they want to be entertaining, to cause a reaction in an audience, or to earn credibility with friends and peers. Other times, choices about what story to tell and how to tell it are simply based on a preconceived idea of what a "good" story should be. These are all powerful forces that motivate authors and shape a project's outcome, but they may also result in projects that aren't as accurate, fair, or effective as they could potentially be.

Deciding which story to tell is a process that involves alignment of your learning objectives with the personal and social needs of your students. But great stories don't have to compromise on either content or fun. Instead, we can view the process of choosing what story to tell as a creative challenge, and approach it from a place of responsibility and

respect for the subject, our audiences, and scientific and historical fact.

Align student passion and curiosity with curricular goals by emphasizing research techniques that rely on credible sources; faithfulness to the inquiry process and scientific method; and providing context by sharing exemplars from professional and student storytellers around the world.

Use these additional criteria to provide transparency and guide student decision-making around the story selection process:

✦ **Purpose.** Develop a class or school-wide mission statement around the purpose and goals of story projects and ensure they align with these agreed-upon values.

✦ **Resources.** Do we have the right tools, talent, or time to do justice to this topic?

✦ **Timeliness.** Does a story topic address a topical issue or help the audience make sense of something happening right now in our local or global community?

# How to Develop a Storytelling Mission Statement

Help guide student decision-making and provide transparency about assessment by developing a set of class guidelines for storytelling. Develop this alongside students to create a shared purpose and increase buy-in. Create a poster of these values to hang in your room and post online for your audience to see.

## Purpose

✦ What kinds of stories should we strive to tell (what are our goals)?

✦ What should our stories strive to accomplish for our audience? (How do our stories help others?)

## Expectations

✦ What are some expectations our audience has about the accuracy and quality of our stories? How do quality and accuracy affect our credibility?

✦ How do our stories push the audience's thinking into new territory?

## Storyteller Ethics

✦ What is the perception we want others to have about us and our stories?

✦ What should we do when we make an error in our storytelling?

✦ What's another way to look at this? What perspectives haven't been included?

✦ Is it okay to talk about other people's experiences without hearing from them directly?

✦ **Originality.** How does your story provide new information or perspectives that your audience can't get elsewhere or hasn't already heard?

✦ **Diversity and representation.** Good scientists and journalists know that large sample sizes and multiple perspectives help us more accurately triangulate the truth. Ask your students and yourself: What are we missing? Who haven't we heard from yet? There are always more than two sides of a story.

## Practical Advice from Storytellers

Here's some great advice I've received over the years about how to keep student projects on track:

✦ Ela Ben-Ur, creator of the Innovators' Compass, often prompts her clients to ask this question when making choices about which direction to take their work: "What matters most?"

✦ Artist and experimental letterer Chris Campe, whose work makes connections between artistic innovation and questioning social conventions to improve society, encourages us to question the status quo by asking: "Does it have to be this way?"

✦ When determining how to keep students from simply chasing popularity with their stories, veteran high school journalism teacher Jack Kennedy recommends asking students: "How does this help anyone?"

# PART II

# WHY USE STORYTELLING TO SUPPORT LEARNING

In part I, we talked about what digital storytelling is and how it works. In part II, we'll look at how storytelling projects can build on what educators already do best to solve problems faced by everyone in our learning communities. This includes leveraging student curiosity to motivate kids and increase engagement, making interdisciplinary connections within our curriculum and to our students' lives, and how to use story projects as an authentic, equitable, and uncheatable form of assessment.

# CHAPTER 7

# WHY DO WE NEED STORYTELLING?

*Storytelling is a tool for knowing who we are and what we want.*

**—Ursula K. Le Guin**

The act of creating stories can be a clarifying process—a way to organize one's thinking and provide transparency around learning. This is as true for our students as it is for other stakeholders. In this chapter, I discuss how storytelling helps connect learning to our students' lives and can even help strengthen our communities.

## How Storytelling Helps All Stakeholders

It takes a village to educate a child, and student-created story projects can help teachers, administrators, and parents solve challenges and create a learning community that is supportive of these kinds of learning experiences.

## Teachers

Teachers use storytelling all the time through direct instruction or when communicating with parents via emails and newsletters. Increasingly, we're also responsible for teaching a host of new curriculum including digital literacy, cultural awareness, and social-emotional wellness, all of which can be accomplished when students learn through the digital storytelling process.

We can use digital stories to:

✦ provide authentic assessment

✦ motivate and inspire students

✦ connect our curriculum to our communities and current events

✦ build a positive class culture

✦ develop student independence, responsibility, and confidence

✦ help students become collaborative problem solvers

## School Leadership

Sharing student-created stories also helps administrators, learning coaches, and board members tell the story of their school and the strengths of their community by:

✦ celebrating successes

✦ providing transparency about curriculum and learning spaces

✦ building community and sharing best practices

## Parents

As partners in learning, parents increasingly look to schools to help their kids develop skills and mindsets beyond the curriculum. Digital story projects provide opportunities to support these goals, such as:

✦ physical and emotional safety

✦ a sense of belonging and confidence

✦ academic rigor

✦ excitement for learning

✦ development of independent thinkers and constructive citizens

✦ digital·literacy

✦ development of personal voice

✦ preparation for work or college

## How Storytelling Helps Learners

Students have many reasons for creating stories in their personal lives, which are generally tied to identity, trying to make sense of the world, and creating a sense of belonging. When we embrace storytelling in academic settings, we acknowledge the desire for students to consume and create stories and provide the professional support students need to develop a healthy relationship to the tools and processes they're already exploring beyond the classroom. Researchers have found that the storytelling process improves intellectual abilities (Alvarez-Mendoza, et al., 2018), and even helps them perform better on tests like Advanced Placement (Saavedra et al., 2021).

Storytelling provides opportunities for students to:

✦ ask questions or satisfy curiosity

✦ process a personal challenge/difficulty

✦ share knowledge and inspire others

✦ make connections to others and build community

✦ have a sense of ownership and control over their lives (self-determination)

✦ foster a sense of empathy and understanding for others

✦ develop a portfolio used for college or work applications

## Purpose

As students or teachers, we have often been asked to work on assignments that go nowhere other than the recycling bin and that no one other than a teacher or administrator sees. And each time we ask ourselves, "What's the point?" If we expect our students to take our lessons and curriculum seriously, then we need to give our students serious assignments.

Project-based learning experiences like digital storytelling answer this question because stories by their very nature are created to have an impact on an audience. Since we're asking our students to put in the hard work and critical thinking to complete our assignments, it might as well be useful to someone! Here are some ways student stories can provide purpose beyond their own personal learning:

✦ share success stories in your classroom and school

✦ seek solutions to challenges in our local and global community

✦ learn from others by providing new perspectives

## Agency

Inviting students to take ownership of their learning through digital storytelling enhances buy-in and helps students make personal connections to our curriculum (Lee & Hannafin, 2016). Treating students as narrative designers and authors rather than passive recipients of knowledge frames their effort as one that has value and creates a sense of responsibility to the material and to the audiences of their work.

## Relevance

When students aren't in class, they learn the way most of us do: by watching YouTube videos, viewing social media posts, and talking with friends. While learning through traditional research methods is important, it's also vital to embrace the tools and knowledge-sharing methods that are now standard for businesses, journalists, politicians, and even teachers!

Embracing digital tools for learning helps us to:

✦ stay relevant in the eyes of our students

✦ develop digital literacy and media literacy skills

✦ provide safe, professional, ethical guidance about how to use these tools

✦ prepare students for future success in college and the workplace

## Authenticity

Tests and worksheets can be like academic training wheels that at first seem like a good way to keep students on track, but when left on too long, they can leave them inexperienced in the art of staying intellectually upright. Storytelling projects facilitate the development of intellectual capacity and resilience precisely because they require each project to stand on its own in the wild of the real world.

## Build Community

We often think of authorship as a solitary activity. While this can be true, stories—like all academic, scientific, and creative work—happen within the context of communities large and small. When we use storytelling projects to frame learning, it provides opportunities to connect with others by:

✦ fostering stronger relationships to the content through the personal choices students make when creating the story, helping them understand their role in and relationship to the topic

✦ sharing knowledge, celebrating successes, and helping local and global communities solve problems

✦ developing community standards for content and quality, and learning ethical decision-making and how to work productively in teams

✦ discovering how to build and see the value of a personal learning network

# Karrin Burns

Karrin Burns, Independent International Educator, Oak Park, Illinois

**Your third graders produced a podcast series, mostly in teams as a self-directed project. Why did you do that, and how did it change the dynamic of learning in your classroom?**

Self-directed learning is vital to students' intellectual and social development, and I've always believed in the power of storytelling because it allows students to make choices, create their own questions, and seek answers. They grow as learners with the capacity to not only tell their own story but listen to and empathize with others.

I implemented a period during each day called "Inquiry and Exploration," and we spent a lot of time spit-balling ideas about what they wanted to learn within the context of our classroom mission statement. We found that most people wanted to do something to help others, and the learners chose to produce a podcast called *The Chat with Mrs. Burns's Third Grade*.

Each week, the podcast team identified a question they wanted to explore, then found and contacted a guest and scheduled an interview. Then, they had to produce a show to answer their question. Learners would have to pitch their ideas to the team for discussion and determine the most thoughtful questions. Once they agreed on a topic and guest, they had to pitch their idea and questions to me for approval.

They were used to curriculum being predecided and static, so I spent a lot of time listening and mentoring, helping them organize, negotiate, and narrow down choices. I let them experience great success as well as failure (which was difficult!) so they knew which they preferred.

Although inquiry and exploration were guided and assessed by Illinois's social studies standards, the curriculum was interdisciplinary. My learners became capable of not only carrying out inquiries about things they were interested in, but they became true collaborators, improved their communication skills, and learned how to really take charge of their own learning. They did the work because they were incredibly interested in it, not because they had to.

**What advice would you give to teachers who are thinking of using storytelling for assessment (emotional support as well as any logistical advice)?**

Always base learning goals on the state standards if that is expected in your district. For example, part of our Grade 3 Illinois Learning Standards is devoted to developing questions, planning inquiries, evaluating sources, using evidence to communicate, and taking action. I could not accomplish that by reading a textbook and taking unit tests, which was what our district was doing at the time. But we can accomplish this and better prepare learners for their futures by allowing students to explore their own curiosity and create experiences that represent their learning.

Consistent formative assessments and feedback are necessary to keep everyone learning and on target. Assessments should include observations, artifacts/products, individual conferencing, and even self-assessment, which is powerful. Be creative and flexible as the teacher and adapt to a learner's idea to ensure adherence to the standards.

**Additional advice:**

✦ Be explicit and transparent with parents and colleagues about what kids are learning and what and how you assess.

✦ Garner support from administration and parents.

✦ Be intentional and clear with students about what and how you're assessing, and what success looks like.

✦ Practice open discussion with learners about their ideas, expectations, and how they can get their message across successfully.

✦ Teacher guidance is key to successful inquiry and exploration.

✦ Encourage our learners to experiment with ways that they find effective.

✦ Be brave! Give up some of the control over how/what is being learned. It's not easy to guide this kind of learning, but it is far more fulfilling, and we experienced excellent outcomes.

**FIGURE 7.1 Podcasting is elementary:** *Karrin Burns' third graders produced a monthly podcast on big ideas and important questions.*

# CHAPTER 8

# STORYTELLING FOR INQUIRY AND DESIGN THINKING

*We make the world significant by the courage of our questions and the depth of our answers.*

**—Carl Sagan**

You've probably noticed by now that the process of publishing stories sounds very familiar. In fact, it relies upon tried-and-true learning processes that we use in the classroom every day. This chapter looks at how to use digital storytelling as a form of inquiry and how narrative design shares the same processes and mindsets that one might use in science, art, and STEM classes.

## A Quest for Understanding

As mentioned earlier, storytelling, like learning, begins and ends with wonder. When we use digital storytelling projects as the schema through which our students experience our curriculum, it makes the process of learning more natural and familiar. And research shows that leveraging students' natural sense of curiosity ultimately leads to more effective learning (Gruber et al., 2014).

## Storytelling as Inquiry-Based Learning

Wonder and inquiry drive the plot of every story and increase our engagement because we want to know the answers to important questions: Will Dorothy find her way back to Kansas? Will Luke and the Rebel Alliance defeat the evil Empire? In the same way, the mysteries of literature, science, society, and the natural world drive learning forward as students seek answers to questions as they complete story projects (Lehne et al., 2015).

Nonfiction stories engage our natural sense of curiosity and provide a vehicle for us to discover answers to our questions. As students seek to answer these questions, they develop the skills and knowledge we want for them, and they often don't even realize they're learning them. They're so caught up in the excitement of creating their purpose-driven project that their learning doesn't even seem like work!

## Science as Storytelling

I've had an intense wonder about the universe ever since I watched the original *Cosmos* TV series in fifth grade. Even though I never became a scientist, I use the scientific method all the time to help me as an artist and writer, and with my students when creating their own work. Storytelling, like science, is about observing the world, asking questions about it, and finding answers or creating solutions (McLeish, 2019).

The similarities between science and the liberal arts are striking:

✦ Even in literature, we use vocabulary from science, such as "catalyst" and "test."

✦ Where science tests phenomena of the physical world, stories are experiments in ideas, dreams, and possibilities.

✦ Like scientists, artists and authors often ask the questions "What if?" "Why not?" and "How come?"

## Living History: Using Documentaries to Make Sense of the Past, Present, and Future

*My knowledge is only as large as the bus window . . .*
**—Miriam Sachs, *There Is Light***
**(quote from the student documentary below)**

**FIGURE 8.1**
**Science is story:**
*The parallels between the scientific method and story structure.*

| SCIENTIFIC METHOD | STORY STRUCTURE |
|---|---|
| Observe a phenomenon in the world and ask a question about it | The status quo, or understanding the world as it has been |
| Create a hypothesis based on research | Inciting incident; a catalyst that initiates the story |
| Test the hypothesis | Rising action, where the protagonist is tested |
| Analyze data | Climax; ultimate test of character |
| Draw conclusions | Resolution, where we learn a lesson or acquire new knowledge |

Like Harvard Graduate School of Education's Project Zero, which advocates for a "see, think, wonder" model of inquiry-based learning, story projects invite students to observe the world, think about what's happening, and ask questions about it. Projects like documentaries, journalism, and explainer videos adopt this same approach to tell stories based on historical fact, and they help students make connections between personal observations in their communities and life with research from credible sources in order to make sense of the past and present.

Generate ideas for historical story projects with questions like:

✦ What are the root causes of our current situation?

✦ What cultural, political, artistic, and scientific conditions led to our situation now?

✦ What are some ways we can solve these challenges?

*Find out how to produce student documentaries in chapter 12.*

# Journalism: STEM for the Humanities

There is no greater way to motivate students than when they look for answers to questions that affect their family, friends, and community. Journalistic stories fulfill this need to find solutions to problems and celebrate successes through a lens of objectivity.

Traditionally, students are encouraged to express themselves through stories by centering their personal worldview and experience—a concept that seems noble but can have the effect of elevating a singular perspective above others, limiting their ability to gain perspective and discouraging contextual knowledge. The social and political result of this mindset is that we develop a culture where we miss each other in translation and have difficulty agreeing on basic facts. Journalism stories require students to think and act in a way they are rarely, if ever, asked to do, which is to seek the advice of experts, present multiple credible perspectives, and embrace objectivity as the central ethical guideline.

**FIGURE 8.2** *Experiential learning projects—like this documentary produced by my students in Vietnam— lead to deeper understanding of history and help students make personal connections to the material. See a link to the documentary in the Digital Resources. (Courtesy of Miriam Sachs.)*

**CASE STUDY**
# Video Documentary as Inquiry Project

One of the most successful projects my students ever made is a documentary produced while on a class trip to Vietnam. Prior to travel, my students Miriam and Paul selected a topic—the religion and spirituality of Vietnam—and researched and prepared to record interviews during our one-week stay. They shot hours of footage and recorded interviews with grandmothers, students, a former Viet Cong officer, and a Buddhist monk.

While editing the footage, they struggled to make sense of all the ideas and concepts and realized that as outsiders, they had difficulty doing justice to the concepts they set out to explore. What started as a straightforward report transformed into a powerful essayistic reflection on the limits of knowledge. Without having studied epistemology, these students came to understand—to feel—the limits of what they could know, and as a result, developed a humbleness toward learning and knowledge, and a new appreciation for how they relate to the world and other people. On top of it all, Miriam, an award-winning poet, wrote the voiceover as long-form poetry, adding yet another layer of personal connection to an already interdisciplinary learning experience.

This wasn't the intent of the assignment—I was teaching filmmaking, not history or philosophy. But the experience was transcendent for my students because this sustained storytelling project allowed them the flexibility to follow their passions wherever it took them and gave us all unexpected and surprisingly moving results.

While Miriam and Paul had prior training and natural talent, the project was successful for a variety of other reasons, too. The intrinsic motivation of exploring a topic they cared about kept them going as they worked on the project for weeks. The experience of learning in a place outside of school, of meeting and working alongside other people, made the learning real and tangible. The struggle to make sense of ideas and convey them clearly to an audience helped them make intellectual and emotional connections not possible with other forms of learning.

Schools often emphasize facts and skills, but what students really need is understanding—of other people, of the world, and of their relationship to it. Experiential story projects like this one help kids develop that understanding. I realize that it may not be feasible to travel far to make documentaries, but people and cultures from other countries are often as close as the other side of your town. And while it may seem like a luxury to spend this much time on projects like this, it's well worth the effort to develop cultural literacy and empathy for others that our world sorely needs right now.

Like scientists and engineers who look to reliable data and facts to draw conclusions and produce solutions to problems, journalists do the same thing with social and political challenges. Journalism is a truly interdisciplinary curriculum where students put civics into action, deploy the skills of language and writing, and craft messages using design techniques from visual arts.

*See resources for journalism curriculum in appendix C.*

# Seeing is Believing: Experiential Learning

In the same way you can't learn to swim by reading a book, the best way to understand any concept is through experience: being a participant or a witness to something in the real world. Research shows that experiential learning—learning by doing—is one of the best ways to create learning that lasts, (Summers & Dickinson, 2012; Koparan & Guven, 2014). When this extends to experiences beyond the classroom, such as field trips or community projects, it creates further opportunities to create empathy for the people, cultures, and ecosystems affected by a topic of study.

Experiential learning is much more than a fun field trip or one-off project. It can become part of your class culture where students conduct research and become inspired by their daily interactions with other people and environments beyond the classroom. Experiential learning elevates learning by providing:

✦ personal connections to the curriculum

✦ context and interdisciplinary connections

✦ opportunities for students to apply their knowledge and skills

✦ a way for students to extend learning by organically creating their new questions of their own

✦ clarity about how their projects can have a real impact on others

# How to Ask the Right Questions

*Wisdom often ends in a question mark, not an exclamation point.*

**—Adam Grant**

A good story, like research, begins with asking the right questions. But how can students do this when they don't know what they don't know?

Questions play a vital role throughout the storytelling creation process. Here are some tips for how to ask the right questions.

✦ During research, identify the most surprising, unusual, or unknown facts and develop questions about those findings.

✦ Refer to your class mission statement or the assignment's goals, both of which remind us about our purpose and help guide question development.

✦ Check yourself by asking: What am I missing? What's another way to look at this?

✦ Don't overlook the obvious: Who haven't I heard from yet? If a story affects a particular group of people and your students are not part of that group, they need to conduct empathy interviews with those stakeholders first.

# The Courage to Ask Good Questions

An inquiry mindset means having the courage to admit that we have more to learn and the strength to ask questions of others, even if it's not always comfortable to do so. Gather the courage to ask questions through these practices:

✦ Reflect on your purpose. Why is this important? What's at stake? How will others benefit by you asking these questions? What would happen if you didn't find the answers to your question?

✦ Have a script. Students should be ready to explain the purpose of their project to others as they ask questions, conduct research, and publish stories.

✦ Practice. Have students interview one another to gain experience and confidence by learning what it's like to ask and respond to questions.

## Keep Projects on Track with Focus Statements

In the same way scientists use a hypothesis to provide direction for research, and writers use thesis statements to structure an essay, authors of digital stories use *focus statements* as driving questions their projects strive to answer. Once research is complete, have students develop narrow focus statements that guide decisions throughout the storytelling process.

*FIGURE 8.3 Stay focused:*
*Stories can suffer from being too broad or vague. Narrow the scope of stories and keep the workflow efficient by developing a focus statement, a question that each story strives to answer.*

## Solutions-Based Learning: Storytelling as Design Thinking

Engineers, app developers, and entrepreneurs all use the design thinking process to create a product or system that solves a problem or addresses a need. We're already familiar with design thinking in STEM, science, and art classes to develop a tangible artifact, but storytelling uses the same process to develop ideas and answers to questions, making it an ideal way to structure the learning process.

| BROAD TOPIC | FOCUS STATEMENT |
| --- | --- |
| How to use literary devices | What are some famous examples of allusion in literature, poetry, and film? |
| Why would I use math if I'm not an engineer or scientist? | How do visual artists use math when creating their work? |
| The role of athletics in our everyday lives | How does exercise affect our mental health? |

56

# Developing a Focus Statement

One of my favorite projects is the public service announcement, where students create a video to advocate for a positive change in audience behavior. In this example, I challenged my students to create a PSA about climate change, and this was the result for one of my students. After running through the storytelling process outlined in chapter 5, she developed a successful focus statement through these steps:

1. Topic assigned: Climate Change

2. Initial student questions: What causes climate change? How can we stop it?

3. Research and exploration: Determine causes of climate change and ways to reduce carbon emissions.

4. Initial ideas for a focus statement: What are some ways that you or I can take action? What can we do to combat climate change that isn't too overwhelming for most people?

5. Final focus statement: Why should we use compact fluorescent light bulbs in our homes?

## What is Design Thinking?

Design thinking is the idea of taking a problem that affects people—like the need for fuel-efficient cars, how to share accurate information for public health campaigns, or even how to make lunch lines move faster—and then designing solutions to that problem using a step-by-step process. The Stanford d.school is famous for using and promoting this design-thinking workflow. This is also the same process we use to develop stories.

+ empathize

+ define

+ ideate

+ prototype

+ test

## Who Is This Story For?

The heart of design thinking involves creating a product that meets the specific needs of a particular end user. In storytelling, that end user is the target audience. Just as advertisers craft messages that use demographic knowledge of a group of people to make ads with the biggest impact, student authors should identify a narrow, specific group of people they are creating their story for, so they can make informed choices about content and style that will resonate with that audience. Having a target audience makes a story more effective and requires students to get to know and empathize with people who may be different from themselves.

# How to Integrate Storytelling as Design Thinking in Your Classroom

Students often create some kind of project, report, or presentation during the year. Try turning one of these traditional assignments into a digital story design thinking challenge.

| CURRICULUM | INQUIRY/DESIGN THINKING CHALLENGE |
|---|---|
| ELA | Community literacy campaign to increase awareness of authors of diverse backgrounds |
| Social Studies | Projects about unknown history in your community |
| Math | Data visualization project to debunk myths, rumors, or conspiracy theories |
| Art | Portraits project that collects images of people throughout your community and tells their stories |

**FIGURE 8.4** *Story as design challenge: Ideas for story projects in every subject area.*

| STEPS OF DESIGN THINKING | STEPS OF STORYTELLING |
|---|---|
| Empathize (who are you designing for?) | Identify the audience and stakeholders: Research and observation, empathy interviews |
| Define (craft an actionable problem statement) | Focus statement, story themes |
| Ideate (idea generation) | Brainstorm topics <br> Create story pitches |
| Prototype (design working models) | Story outlines and scripts <br> Create storyboards |
| Test | Story drafts <br> Rough cuts of video and podcast stories |

**FIGURE 8.5** *Designing stories: The similarities between design thinking and storytelling.*

# PSA as Design Thinking

In the public service announcement project discussed above, my student wanted to create a video story that would motivate her peers to take actionable steps to help reduce carbon emissions, and therefore reduce the impact of climate change. Here is her design thinking process.

1. **Empathize.** To make good choices throughout the storytelling process, she spoke with her target audience (teens in the U.S.) to find out what they knew about the topic, what motivated them to take climate-reducing actions or not, and what kinds of stories they liked to watch or listen to. These empathy interviews went a long way in determining the final storyline, her decision to use humor, who to cast as actors, and how she'd define the problem to be solved.

2. **Ideate.** After conducting research about the topic and comparing those findings to what she knew about the target audience, she developed a story pitch (see chapter 5).

3. **Prototype.** Watching sample commercials and PSAs inspired her vision for what the story eventually became, and she developed the first draft of a script.

4. **Test Round 1:** The first draft of a script was workshopped in class, and after receiving feedback from me and her classmates, was revised for clarity and effectiveness.

5. **Test Round 2:** Once the script was completed, she worked with a team of classmates to record video footage, which was also given feedback as it arrived.

6. **Test Round 3:** After the video clips were edited and graphics and music were added, a complete version of the PSA was screened for feedback. The students made minor technical adjustments and recorded additional footage to clarify the message and story. A final cut of the project was delivered for publishing and grading.

*Learn more about PSA projects in chapter 14.*

**FIGURE 8.6** *This student's PSA project was successful because she used the design thinking process. The project ultimately won a national award.*

**TEACHER PROFILE**
# Dan Ryder

Dan Ryder, Design Facilitator at Community Regional Charter School in Skowhegan, Maine, a regional PK–12 public charter school district

**Why is it important to have an end user in mind when designing assignments for students?**

I emphasize with my learners that I'm teaching them to apply a given design process and mindset. Having an end user in mind for design challenges isn't just good pedagogy, it's also highly practical. The number of times learners ask, "Why are we doing this?" has lessened with each design challenge, and students realize that we create in the service of authentic problems and users.

**How has the iterative process (prototype/test/revise) been helpful for student learning in your classroom?**

The learners who progress most in my seminars aren't the ones with the prettiest products or the best ideas in the room. They're the ones who practice metacognition and talk about what they are learning, the choices they are making, and why they are making them. They are the ones that listen to feedback. These learners make a conscious decision to apply the feedback or remix it into an insight they can make into something rad. I think it's also okay for them to look at their work and acknowledge there are opportunities for leveling up—always.

Challenging learners with a steady stream of meaningful, actionable feedback has helped them realize that learning isn't about arbitrary due dates and averaging two grades to determine what you "got" for that project. It's about making something that matters and improving upon it all along because that's how learning happens: constantly.

**How do you make time and space for editing and revision?**

It's a constant challenge, but planning backward helps tremendously. I know how long they have to deliver evidence of understanding, and where I want my learners to arrive, in terms of the skills and knowledge I want them to demonstrate through the design process.

Documenting matters. Keeping track of growth over time matters. Taking lots of screenshots and photos of sketches and doodles matters. Talking and conferencing about edits, changes, new understandings, and realization matters.

**What advice do you have for teachers integrating the design thinking process in their classrooms?**

Start small. If we use that basic premise of "How might we . . .?" to structure our projects and assessments, we can turn any activity or project into a more human-centered design experience.

It's about learning content, skill development, and growth through the design process—not just the end product. I have a learner right now working on a social-emotional health video game design that will likely not reach a playable prototype stage. However, because they have shared their progress and thinking with me daily in short conferences and I've taken loads of pictures of their evidence, I feel confident I'll be able to assess the depth of their understanding.

# CHAPTER 9
# STORYTELLING AS ASSESSMENT

I've always struggled to find a good way to assess my students, and as far as I can tell, it's everyone's least favorite part of teaching. How can we get an accurate sense of student achievement, discourage cheating, encourage productive behavior, and satisfy the requirements of state standards, as well as the demands of administrators and parents who expect grades and high test scores?

This chapter explores ways to use digital stories as a form of assessment that are meaningful, purposeful, and equitable; what to consider when designing storytelling projects for assessment; and ideas for how you might grade storytelling projects themselves.

## Why Use Storytelling for Assessment?

*If you can't explain it simply, you don't understand it well enough.*

**—Albert Einstein**

Storytelling helps address many challenges of traditional assessments by sidestepping their traps: "common" evaluations where all students are expected to have the same answers or similar outcomes; time constraints that don't make space for individual learning needs; and grading students with criteria that are inflexible and don't account for curiosity and intellectual creativity. There are many reasons why story projects are a great form of assessment:

✦ Because each story project is original and authentic, students are less able and willing to cheat.

✦ Having to explain and apply concepts within a unique context requires a much deeper, more meaningful and nuanced understanding of concepts than traditional forms of assessment (Boaler, 1997).

✦ Authentic publication of stories provides a level of public accountability for student work, including the development of portfolios which are increasingly used by colleges and employers.

✦ When students are passionate about their projects and care about the outcome, it disincentivizes cheating.

## Uncheatable: Evidence-Based Assessment

Tests are vulnerable to cheating, and text can be easily plagiarized or written with AI bots. But digital stories require students to provide evidence of their knowledge, either by documenting it with images, sound, and video, or through the creation of an original artifact that can only be made with the application of knowledge through their specific experience. Because each student's project is unique, digital stories offer a potentially uncheatable form of assessment.

## Agency and Engagement

Student-created stories invite students to explain their reasoning and share their process, creating a culture that honors individual perspectives and choices. More importantly, it provides a purpose for the assessment beyond just a grade. Students know their hard work will have an impact on others, thereby increasing investment in the process and outcome.

## Equity and Learning Modalities

While it's often important to have common assessments so that students have foundational knowledge (for example, a type of writing or applying a specific equation to solve a problem), our assessments can often get in the way of understanding what students know.

Students who are shy, for example, may falter in class presentations or Socratic seminars, and students who are writers with a more methodical pace

(like me!) may appear weak simply because it takes them longer to organize and craft their thoughts. Students with learning disabilities, many of which may be undiagnosed, can also struggle to demonstrate knowledge simply because they struggle with the tools we use to measure achievement.

Story projects provide multiple options for students to explain themselves, letting them use the medium and techniques that best allow them to showcase what they know.

# How to Use Storytelling to Assess Student Knowledge

There are several ways students might tell the story of their learning journey and show what they know: as an original work that covers new material, as an anthology of their learning (portfolio), or as self-reflection. The first two ways are covered in part III of this book, which offers a collection of different types of projects. In the following section, I'll talk specifically about self-reflection. All story projects can be used as either formative assessments during a unit, or as a culminating activity for summative assessment.

## Self-Reflection

The quickest and easiest way to provide meaningful assessment is to have students explain what they've learned in their own words (Marzano, 2009). This can be shared privately with the teacher or publicly with their audience through online stories. Sharing publicly allows for transparency of the process and can help earn respect from their audience, peers, and teacher.

# Jodie Deinhammer

Jodie Deinhammer, secondary science educator, Coppell, Texas

**You taught your first year of high school anatomy and physiology without giving tests. Why did you do that, and how were you able to assess students in ways that were accurate, equitable, and meaningful?**

On the first day of school last year, one of my students suggested we have no tests. At first, I kind of laughed about it but then thought, why not? I discovered that it was so much more fun to design curriculum that way. I intentionally incorporated more formative assessments to let me see who knew what, but at no risk to students or their grades. It helped me know what needed to be reviewed or clarified, and it built kids' confidence.

**What does storytelling mean to you in the context of a science classroom, and how did you use storytelling as part of your assessment of students?**

In science, storytelling is often based on data and how our students make sense of it, and also in ways that help the public understand. For example, "How can we use the evidence and results in our lab to help convince people to make better choices regarding their health and wellness?"

I developed different methods of assessing learning, like students taking pictures during the lab and annotating the organs and structures. It turned out to be a bit more challenging for them than tests because they had to justify their thinking. A side benefit was that they began comparing images and annotations to those made by other groups—their conversations were way beyond my expectations.

At the end of the marking period, I asked them to create a sketchnote, graphic organizer, or product of their choice to demonstrate what they had learned using evidence from labs completed in class.

**What advice would you give to teachers who are thinking of using storytelling for assessment?**

I would suggest trying this approach in one marking period or unit of study. The preplanning is the most important part for me, and I believe it's important to start with the end in mind: What are my objectives, and what do I want students to master or know by the end of this unit?

I use a lot of formative assessments throughout the unit, each day trying to check what they know. By doing these types of quick checks each day, the repetition helps them retain the information long term.

CHAPTER 9
Storytelling as Assessment

## WRITTEN REFLECTIONS

Explain your thinking through text, such as:

✦ **Blog or social media posts.** Sharing one's learning publicly elevates the quality of the reflection and can help others learn from students' successes and mistakes.

✦ **Learning journals.** This is a document shared confidentially with the teacher to provide clarity on the learning process, including team dynamics.

✦ **Artist statement.** Explaining the intent and creative/intellectual process to an audience shows respect for learners as professionals who have an important perspective to share. This also helps teachers gain insight into students' thought processes.

## MULTIMEDIA REFLECTIONS

Use digital storytelling tools to tell the story of learning.

✦ **Audio notes.** Students use native audio recording apps on mobile devices to create a thoughtful reflection—a great option for students with limited writing abilities.

✦ **Process videos.** Create time-lapse or other types of videos showing students producing their projects.

✦ **Blog post.** Students create a multimedia post on their digital portfolio or class website that includes text and documentation, such as photos or video of their project.

✦ **Digital portfolios.** A personal website or digital book where students collect their completed learning artifacts, including reflections.

**FIGURE 9.1** *My journalism student created a blog post on our publication website to reflect on her experience making a documentary about former gang members. Public forms of self-reflection provide transparency, build trust and respect for the journalist, and provide a purpose for the self-assessment.*

**FIGURE 9.2** *My student Kamyjah Blackwell created this digital book to explore and process racism that students of color face in our community. The photography is enhanced with text, and audio recordings of interviews with her subjects. Also included is an audio personal reflection about what she learned through the process.*

# LIVING IN THE SHADOWS

**THE AUTHOR'S MESSAGE TO YOU**

I am Kamyjah Blackwell a 11th grader at Mira Costa. Although these stories are not mine, I want you to hear them because people you know face things like this all the time.

As a person of color, throughout my life I have seen how people who are not of color get the spotlight. In many instances, people of white shades opinions are heard over ours. Or, when we feel strongly about something they find a way to invalidate it. In many instances we start to adjust ourselves, and adapt to the way people treat us, it is time to hold them accountable. Also, how within our community we degrade one another, whether it is colorism or LGBTQ-ism. I think that this has led many people of color to feel like they have to sit back and let the people "meant" to shine based off societal standards shine. So in this book, I am showing the impact this has on many people of color. Also demonstrating how no people of any color should have to stand in ones shadow to shine.

# Triangulate Student Growth with Stakeholder Evaluations

Who gets to evaluate student work? Often, it's just the teacher. But our view is limited, and to create a more meaningful, authentic, and nuanced picture of student learning, it makes sense that we involve stakeholders like teammates, who got to see the learning up close, and even the end user of the product—the audience—to check for effectiveness.

## The Four Dimensions of Evaluation

Moving outward from the personal to the public, feedback from each of these stakeholder groups provides social context and creates an awareness of how a student's work affects others—the true measurement of any project-based learning experience, especially stories.

## SELF-EVALUATION

Self-evaluation makes space for metacognitive processes and quiet, personal reflection on one's own work.

✦ **Public sharing.** Students talk in front of the class during screenings or gallery walks about their choices, obstacles they encountered, and successes, either as a brief presentation, or by responding to on-the-fly questions from the teacher and classmates. This helps all students learn from one another.

✦ **Private sharing.** Students submit confidential, written self-reflections, which allow time for deeper contemplation, and to share thoughts they may not feel comfortable talking about publicly.

## PEER EVALUATION

Because of their similarity in age, and a shared experience with the assignment, there is a specific type of credibility that goes along with peer evaluations that students might not get from other stakeholders. These can be public evaluations shared orally, or through confidentially written comments. They can help to:

✦ **Build excitement.** A gallery walk or film festival screening can become a celebration of achievement, and students can be inspired when they are able to see work created by their peers.

✦ **Evaluation as leadership.** In my journalism class, student editors provide feedback for the work of peers whom they mentor throughout the production process. Ultimately, the quality of work is higher, and students benefit by developing storytelling and leadership skills they'd never get if all projects were evaluated only by the teacher.

✦ **Accountability.** One of the biggest problems with group projects is uneven contributions or interpersonal conflicts. Team meetings and written evaluations keep everyone accountable for their contributions, work ethic, and professionalism.

## TEACHER EVALUATION

Teacher evaluations add a professional perspective, context, and experience to the feedback process.

✦ **Share expert opinions.** Provide your expertise as you share feedback related to technical craft and curriculum accuracy.

✦ **Fill in the gaps.** Younger and inexperienced students often miss technical or social elements of storytelling. Teachers can provide cultural and historical context, and play devil's advocate by asking about alternative creative choices.

✦ **Model the inquiry mindset.** Asking students about their intentions and content and creative choices often reveals their thought process that's not always visible in the final product or self-evaluations.

## AUDIENCE EVALUATION

The true measure of any story is figuring out how well it lands with the audience it was designed for. Consider using feedback from audiences as a truly authentic way to check the effectiveness of student stories.

✦ **Track metrics.** Review data about how many people view or interact with stories on websites, digital books, or social media posts, and in which part of the world the viewers live.

✦ **Get feedback through comments.** Consider leaving the comment feature on for social media and website posts and encourage the audience to ask questions and share their reactions.

✦ **Conduct a survey or poll.** Use tools like Google Forms to get feedback about what the audience likes best about the story. What are their suggestions for future topics?

# Authentic Feedback from YouTube Comments

"Mr. Hernandez, someone left comments about my film on YouTube . . . and I'm not sure what to do."

When Morgan, a sophomore filmmaking student of mine, came to me with this concern, I assumed the worst. But I couldn't have anticipated what came next.

On our storytelling trip to Cuba, she produced a documentary about the challenges faced by the people of that country. Her film was an attempt to reflect on her own experience as an American coming to a communist country for the first time, and how her firsthand knowledge was very different from the narrative about Cubans that appears in American textbooks and our national consciousness. Her film focused on a shared humanity and what we have in common.

It turned out that the comments she received weren't from a troll, but from someone who lived in Cuba, and took issue with her approach. He called out her American privilege that romanticized poverty, and he genuinely wanted her to portray a more accurate story.

After she showed me the viewer's comment, I suggested she reply to explain herself. What transpired was a conversation between my student and a person in another part of the world who had experienced the subject of her project. They ended up coming to an understanding, and Morgan received the best assessment she could ever get: real, authentic feedback from someone who literally lived the story she was trying to tell. This multidimensional assessment that went beyond fact-checking and into ethical and interpersonal growth is an experience no teacher could ever provide.

Publishing one's work publicly opens students up to feedback that may not be as gentle as what a teacher might provide. But as we found out, it provided a valuable learning experience that stuck with my student and her classmates, and it was probably the best way we could come to see the blind spots we all have in our ability to understand the world.

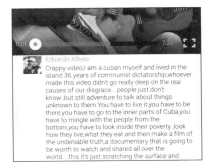

*FIGURE 9.3* *The best feedback should also be authentic—from an audience beyond the classroom. After my student received critical comments on a video she posted on YouTube (left), she engaged in dialogue with the viewer, ultimately coming to appreciate his perspective (right) and gaining a much deeper understanding of the subject.*

# How to Grade Storytelling Projects

Storytelling projects are experiences that add up to much more than the sum of their parts, making evaluation and grading challenging, especially if this type of assignment is new to you. There is no answer key, and rubrics often fail to account for unique circumstances that affect the effort students put into a project and how it turns out. Every teacher has their own grading philosophy, and you'll need to develop a plan that works best for you, your school culture, and your students' developmental abilities. But after 25 years of teaching storytelling, I can vouch for narrative evaluations, which I find to be the most accurate, fair, and helpful for students.

Here are some suggestions as you develop the best evaluation system for your classroom.

## Establish Criteria for Grading

Determine whether you are assessing content, storytelling technique, or both, then establish realistic expectations and requirements for student projects.

### CONTENT

✦ What skills must be demonstrated in the project?

✦ What subject-specific vocabulary, concepts, or definitions need to be included?

✦ Accuracy/clarity of explanation of facts, definitions, and concepts.

✦ Length: How many pages of a book, slides of a presentation, minutes of a video, or number of images are needed to explain the topic?

✦ Which multimedia elements are required?

✦ How will students communicate data (if applicable), like charts or graphs?

✦ What is the expectation for citing research?

### STORYTELLING TECHNIQUE AND CRAFT

✦ Photos and video are technically precise, such as focus and appropriate composition. Audio is clear and audible.

✦ Text is sized appropriately for an average reader.

✦ Writing uses correct grammar and spelling, and the style is appropriate for the medium and audience.

✦ Layout and design are simple and clear, not busy or overwhelming.

✦ Editing of media is smooth, free of glitches, and well-paced.

✦ The organization of information and the story is appropriate for the topic and helps communicate the ideas of this story.

# What to Assess

*If they can get you asking the wrong questions, they don't have to worry about the answers.*
**—Thomas Pynchon**

While it's important for students to be able to define terms and apply concepts, we can also use the evaluation process to encourage the development of constructive behaviors and mindsets, and help students use their learning in a social context.

## Assess Values, Not Systems

Designing an effective assessment comes down to being clear on what we value, because that's where teachers and students will put their energy. The advantage of using story projects for assessment is that they go far beyond the knowledge acquisition of traditional assessments by encouraging the development of attitudes and skills that are important to our students as members of a productive community. Some of these values include:

✦ evaluating sources

✦ how to choose topics of research

✦ originality and innovation

✦ empathy

✦ intellectual and social courage

Consider the mindsets you want to encourage in your students. These are some questions I've used throughout the storytelling process, including assessment:

✦ What challenges did you encounter and what mistakes did you make completing this project?

✦ Which of your assumptions were challenged when you made this project?

✦ How were you inclusive of diverse perspectives and cultural experiences?

✦ How did your collaboration with others (teammates or people outside the classroom) help you complete this project?

✦ What do you still wonder about or are still unsure about (further exploration)?

When everyone is used to scores and letter grades, moving to non-traditional evaluations like these can be challenging because it asks us to reevaluate the purpose of grading. For me, the questions above are *the* most important questions we can ask students to reflect upon because they apply to any future learning experience, and help students see their work as one point within the continuity of their learning, as well as how their projects are part of a larger global narrative.

# PART III

# STORYTELLING PROJECTS

In this section, I'll share some of my favorite storytelling lessons that you can customize to use in your classroom right away. I've organized them by learning mindset, and medium rather than by subject area, because all these lessons are flexible enough to be used in any content area or grade level and are often interdisciplinary. Use these in tandem with previous chapters that provide valuable detail about assessment, insights about forming student teams, the advantages of different media types, and a ton of other information that will lead to a story creation process that is better aligned to your curriculum and make the process more fun.

## How to Use This Section

For each of these projects, I've included examples for beginning storytellers, as well as more complex options to try when your students have more experience. Young students are very capable of creating complex, long-term projects (like the podcast done by third graders, described in chapter 7), so my suggestion is to consider student skill level rather than age alone when determining what kind of projects to use. Where I've included examples from a specific subject area, it's by no means the only curricular area that can use a particular lesson. These are only suggestions to give you a better sense of what's possible.

*See student examples, tools, and other resources for making stories on the website for this book.*

These projects are meant to be a starting point. Modify, customize, and adapt them to meet the needs of your students and classroom culture. With a few exceptions, I've mostly avoided referring to specific tools or apps, since those change frequently. You can see an up-to-date list of tools I like on the book's website.

## Timeframe

The length of time it will take to create a digital story depends on the complexity of the assignment or topic, student experience and skill, and your expectations of quality. Other factors that affect how long it takes to make a story depend on your learning goals. If you're using stories to reflect social changes in the community while your downtown is being remodeled, or creating a student portfolio, the process could take weeks or months before you can be "done" with it. Shorter stories, for example those created with photography or a three-slide explainer video, can be created in a matter of minutes.

# CHAPTER 10
# UNIVERSAL STORY PROJECTS

In this chapter, I outline two of my favorite go-to projects that I find to be the most adaptable to any subject area.

Use these universal story projects to:

✦ provide an alternative to class presentations or essays

✦ check for knowledge and understanding (assessment)

✦ provide flexibility in when and where students work, and provide opportunities to stay productive when not in school (like snow days or remote learning)

## Explainer Videos

You've probably seen many explainers yourself. They're short videos posted on social media or YouTube that explain a concept, define a term, show a process, or advocate a point of view. Typically just a few minutes long, they use images, graphics, video, animation, text, voiceover, and sometimes an on-screen performer or music to convey information and ideas. Although voiceover is often used, explainers rely heavily on visuals like photos, video, infographics, text, and animation.

## Why Use Explainer Videos?

Explainers are the Swiss Army knife of storytelling projects. Literally any topic can be the subject of these kinds of stories. Other advantages include:

✦ creating quick-win, bite-sized stories that can be shared with your community

✦ providing a safe option for students who are shy, or are not great public speakers (yet).

✦ inclusiveness of students with varying abilities, including language learners (just add closed captions!)

✦ scaffolding complex storytelling techniques like story structure, writing, and visual design that can be used later in more complex projects like podcasts or video documentaries

# Does All Media Need to Be Student-Created?

When students create stories, there can be the temptation to just download images, music, graphics, and videos from the internet rather than generate original media. But doing so, even for students working on school projects, is often illegal. To develop ethical digital citizens and avoid violating copyright law, set expectations for what proportion of media needs to be original, and what can be used from royalty-free or public domain sources. If your curricular goals for story projects include having students learn to collect data, meet and interview people, or learn to take photos or record sound or video, it only makes sense that their media should be original, created by them specifically for this project. But there may be times when it's impossible for students to create original media, for example when they need a photo of the earth from space or a historical landmark in another country. In cases like these, use royalty-free sources like Creative Commons or the Library of Congress.

*Find out more about ethical storytelling, including resources for copyright, fair use, and royalty-free media in appendix B.*

Explainers can cover just about any topic, but here are a few ideas to get you started.

+ **Define a concept.** Have students explain an idea or historical background of a topic or vocabulary word from your curriculum, such as confirmation bias, the difference between metaphor and simile, how the stock market works, etc.

+ **How-to video.** Explain how to do something, such as how to register to vote, apply for a scholarship, diagram a sentence, apply a mathematical formula, or set up a science lab.

+ **Dispel myths and rumors.** Have students identify a commonly held misbelief related to your curriculum or from their community, then create a video to debunk those myths. For example, the economic impacts of immigrants, or the misconception that lightning never strikes twice in the same spot.

+ **Origin stories.** Explain the history of a phenomenon from your curriculum. Why is a stop sign an octagon? Why do we drive on the right or left side of the road? How did the Great Lakes form?

Below is a chart comparing simple explainer video topics to more complex ones that might be appropriate for students with more experience and time. The difference between beginner and advanced story projects is usually length and complexity, including technical complexity like animations, video footage, and graphs that might need to be created specifically for the story. To keep from becoming overwhelmed, limit beginners to just a few slides, shorter scripts, and simpler concepts.

| BEGINNER EXPLAINER VIDEO | ADVANCED ALTERNATIVE |
|---|---|
| About Me. Make a 3–5 slide presentation introducing yourself to the class. | Origin Story. Make a presentation about where something or someone came from, or how a social/political/cultural system developed. |
| Definitions. Make a 5–10 slide presentation defining a concept from your curriculum (provide a list of topics for students to choose from). | Complex Definitions. Define a complex concept, such as confirmation bias, or the difference between metaphor and simile. |
| How-To. Create a presentation that explains how to do something in 3–6 steps, such as how to set up or log in to class laptops; how to sign up for a library card; or how to register to vote. | Myth Debunking. Dispel myths, rumors, or conspiracy theories. Provide evidence and research and use reasoning skills to debunk false claims. |

FIGURE 10.1 **Leveling up:** *Explainer video topics for beginner and advanced storytellers.*

# Digital Books

As with explainer videos, the beauty of digital books is their versatility: they are curriculum agnostic and can be used in any grade level and subject area. Digital books can serve the same purposes as traditional books, meaning that they can be created for any topic and genre, from a memoir to a how-to manual to a coffee table art book.

## Why Use Digital Books?

Like explainer videos, digital books allow you to incorporate many kinds of media, collect and curate learning artifacts from other assignments, and present ideas and information in ways that are most effective for the topic. The audience experience with digital books is different from an explainer video, in that readers can set their own pace and decide where to go in the story, jumping to a later chapter, reading definitions in a glossary, or lingering on an image or paragraph of text.

Multimedia elements like video or audio can sit side by side with text to provide context, and the entire book becomes a truly interactive story experience where readers become participants in how those stories unfold. Use digital books instead of websites when you want to have more selectivity and control over distribution of the stories.

Use digital books to create:

+ class or staff manuals
+ anthologies
+ portfolios
+ literary magazines
+ workbooks
+ science lab reports
+ foreign language tourist guides

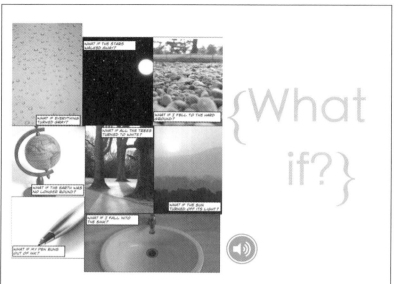

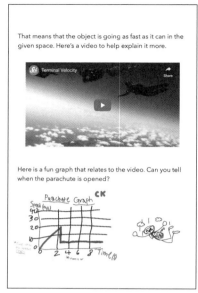

**FIGURE 10.2** *Digital books are a great way for students to share their learning in an authentic way. Students can create books on their own or contribute a section to a larger topic. Elementary student Holly Smith created a poetry book that includes audio of her reading the piece (left), and middle school science students explained a concept with multimedia (right). (Images courtesy Karen Bosch and Leah Lacrosse.)*

**FIGURE 10.3** *My students publish an annual literary magazine, Dilation, that curates creative writing, art, video and spoken word from students around the world. See a link to the magazine in the Digital Resources.*

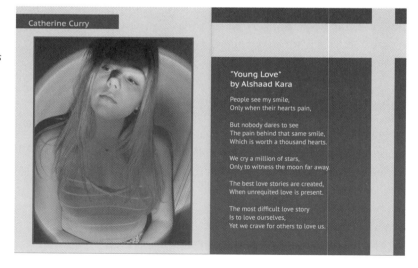

# Steps for Creating an Explainer Video or Digital Book

Although they use different media, explainer videos and digital books use similar processes for authoring. A best practice for any story project is to look to exemplars made by professionals as well as students to inform content, design, and style choices.

## Research the Topic

Thoroughly understand your topic by researching a variety of primary resources, understanding definitions, the people involved, and the historical context for the topic.

## Outline the Story

Organize thoughts and information and create a logical structure for the story with a bulleted outline. Each bullet can be used to create a slide or page, and it can be used as the basis for a voice-over script.

| BEGINNER DIGITAL BOOK IDEAS | ADVANCED DIGITAL BOOK IDEAS |
|---|---|
| How-To Guide. Have students create a three- to five-page book for students or parents that explains how to do a task, such as how to write a persuasive essay, how to log into the school LMS, or how to volunteer at school. | • embed video or explainer videos<br>• create infographic workflow charts |
| Real World Connections. Make a three- to five-page book where students document then explain a phenomenon from your curriculum as seen in their community, such as historical sites, estuaries, engineering applications like bridges, etc. (Provide a list for students to choose from.) | • add animations, maps, or infographics<br>• collaborate with students in other cities or countries |
| Literary Magazine or Academic Journal. Collect student-created stories or research to share with a wider audience. | • add editorial illustrations for each story or chapter<br>• create themed issues to encourage work in a specific area of study |

FIGURE 10.4  **Beginning & advanced book ideas:** How to add depth and sophistication.

## Collect and Create Media

Find and create all the text and multimedia you will need for your story, based on a list generated during the development of the outline. Build in time for students to collect, create, or find media, such as:

✦ illustrations, photos, and video footage

✦ infographics, charts, graphs, and maps

✦ audio, such as interviews, spoken word, or recordings of performances

✦ music (if any)

## Write the Script

Scripts are the backbone of explainer videos and provide much of the information and explanation of the visuals we might see on screen. For digital books, most of the writing will appear as image captions and text boxes that provide context and information, such as historical information or definitions of key concepts. If a digital book uses audio clips, such as spoken word, interviews, or natural sounds, they can be recorded, then embedded as audio widgets.

*Learn more about writing for digital stories in chapter 12.*

## Record, Edit, and Publish

The final phase involves publishing stories in a format that your audience can access. For explainers, this means recording the presentation and then exporting the recording as a video. I prefer screen recording a presentation with apps like Keynote that also have built-in animation tools and recording features.

For digital books, you have the choice of exporting the book in one of two ways: as an EPUB digital book, or simply saved as an editable document in the format of your book authoring software (like Pages or Word). The difference is that EPUB is a universal format that can be read by anyone with an e-reader device or software, no matter what device or software you used to create the book. Doing it this way creates a book that preserves your design and information and allows you to reach the widest audience.

Sharing a book as an editable word processing document is a great option if a) you want to create projects like workbooks, where students or colleagues can add their own text, drawing, or multimedia artifacts, or b) whenever you want to invite users to remix and add on to your initial ideas. While there is an option to export as a PDF, doing so loses most of the functionality of a digital book, such as interactivity and the playback of multimedia.

# CHAPTER 11
# ANTHOLOGY PROJECTS

We're probably most familiar with stories that can stand alone, like novels, movies, reports, and presentations. But we can also use digital stories to collect and curate ideas or evidence—as vessels that contain many smaller stories made by one or many students.

Anthology stories have many uses in the classroom:

✦ Provide context to a topic by making comparisons, sharing links to resources, and showing change over time.

✦ Provide collaboration opportunities by gathering content from a variety of students or those living in multiple locations.

✦ Collect, track, and reflect on student growth and progress.

✦ Activate high-level thinking through curation skills—the art of selection and organization—which is a kind of storytelling in itself, used by museums, literary and scientific journals, and writers of nonfiction books.

In the last chapter, we discussed two major anthology formats, explainer videos and digital books. But there are many other story formats that can help students collect and curate ideas.

## Podcasts

This is a great format to collect expert interviews, audio artifacts, and data, and a chance to hear reactions from those affected by or interested in a particular topic. A single episode can curate ideas around a single topic or person, whereas a podcast series can include as many topics and people as you have time for. This extensibility is infinite and can continue across school years and changes in student enrollment.

## Video Documentaries

After students have experience with explainer videos, try video documentaries, which allow for more complex storytelling by including interviews and visual evidence. The major difference between documentaries and explainers is that documentaries require students to go out into the world and use a video camera and microphone as the primary tool for observation and data collection, whereas explainers are made almost exclusively with presentation software on a computer.

*Find out more about producing documentaries in the next chapter.*

## Websites

We use online stories to get timely information, as a reference resource, and to stay connected to others. Websites function in ways similar to digital books, but they are always online, easily searchable, and can be quickly updated.

## Social Media Stories

Finding your audience where they are and providing quick, timely, digestible bites of information are the key selling points of using social media to tell stories.

Strengths of social media stories include:

✦ **Access.** Social media puts your story and ideas in front of your audience wherever they are. Use hashtags to create searchable posts that can be found by anyone.

✦ **Timeliness.** Social media platforms allow students to publish stories with timely information their audience might need right away, such as results of school elections or game results, or to alert them to event changes like updated times and locations.

✦ **Community.** Let the audience follow along the learning journey as students post updates about a long-term project or the latest events in class.

✦ **Interactivity.** Audience members can comment, ask questions, share with their followers, and engage in online dialogue wherever they may be. Tag other people and organizations to notify them of your post.

# Portfolios

*Projects are the new resume.*

—**Seth Godin**

Collecting student work across a school year is a time-honored tradition. It reveals student progress and allows students to highlight examples of their best work. Creating digital portfolios that are public and accessible to those outside of school heightens the sense of urgency students feel to create meaningful work, and, for older students, opens up opportunities for them to network with professionals and be seen by colleges or future employers, especially when many colleges are moving away from standardized testing as an admissions requirement. Start by using portfolios for assessment and self-reflection, then move toward the concept of portfolios as a type of professional biography and online resume.

Use portfolios for:

✦ student goal setting

✦ assessment and tracking of student progress

✦ resume building

✦ college and job applications

✦ developing a professional learning network (by linking back to projects they have created in class)

Portfolios can take any number of forms, with the most common being websites or digital books. Older students may want to extend their portfolio to include professional social media sites.

**FIGURE 11.1**

***The story of student learning:***
*Portfolios collect artifacts and show the depth and breadth of student learning, revealing growth over time, and providing transparency of the learning process. Older students can use portfolios for job and college applications. In this portfolio, my journalism student included her best video projects, as well as a list of awards (with links) and other accomplishments and reflections.*

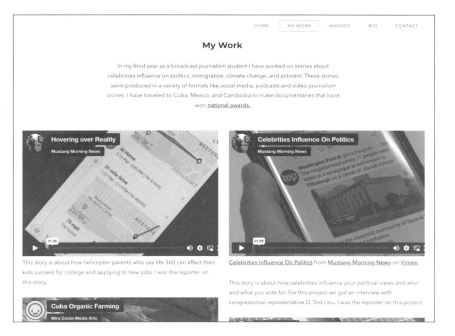

# CHAPTER 12
# STORIES FOR OBSERVATION AND INQUIRY

*The scientist is not a person who gives the right answers, he's one who asks the right questions.*

—Claude Levi-Strauss

We teach students the importance of research all the time, especially quantitative data—numbers and statistics. But one of the most compelling types of research is qualitative data, information we collect through observation and interviews. Also known as rich data, it's used by social scientists, psychologists, and marketing experts to reveal information impossible to detect in quantitative research, and it has the added benefit of requiring our students to get out into the world to interact with other people when doing so.

While all storytelling media can be leveraged for observation, data collection, and inquiry, those highlighted here lend themselves most readily to the inquiry process.

# Photography

The most direct of observation techniques, photography is probably the easiest, fastest, most familiar, and least complex type of digital storytelling. Use it to collect visual evidence and analyze actions and phenomena. I begin every storytelling course with a photography project since it models the entire process in a fast, neat package.

## Annotation Project

One of the easiest and most powerful uses of photography is to have students label, comment on, and describe elements within an image. Using the markup tool on smartphones or tablets, have students identify and label parts of an image. Or use a whiteboard app to add text, links, and multimedia alongside an image to extend audience understanding. Publish and share the annotated images individually, or as part of a larger project like an explainer video, digital book, or social media story.

Use annotation projects to:

✦ label parts of plants or animals in biology

✦ identify parts of sentences, paragraphs, or details of poetry stanzas in language arts

✦ annotate scores in music classes

✦ find bugs or highlight exemplars in lines of code in computer science

✦ label and explain design elements in architecture, painting, or sculpture in visual arts

✦ show processes and label components used in STEM projects

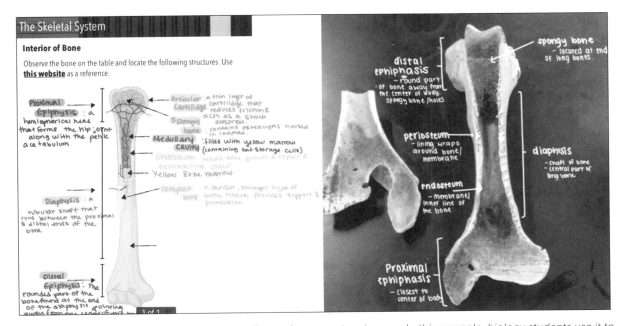

**FIGURE 12.1** *Use markup tools to label, describe, and comment on images. In this example, biology students use it to identify parts of a bone. Image by Saipragnya Akula.*

## Photo Essay: Inquiry through Sequential Observation

Photo essays are the creation and arrangement of multiple photos around a theme or topic, usually published on a website, digital book, or social media account. Add text to these projects to provide detail, context, and facts from research. Use photo series to provide multiple examples of a topic, show changes over time, make connections, and understand historical context, and help students develop a stronger sense of theme and curation and editing skills.

# What's It Take?

**Gear:** Smartphone or tablet with still camera. Publishing platform, such as a digital book, website, or social media account

**Optional:** External microphone, video camera (to record video interviews)

**Time to complete this project:** A few minutes to a few hours

**Other considerations:** Make time to find people to interview, write questions, and publish their responses. Choose lesser-known people who are colorful, well-spoken, and have a unique perspective to share.

Here are some ideas for how you might use photo essays:

✦ **Catalog.** Take 5 to 10 images that document a phenomenon from your curriculum that appears on your campus, in your community, or on a field trip.

✦ **Compare/Contrast.** Collect photos that show similarities or reveal differences by putting images side by side. In science, this might be a comparison of leaf structures. Foreign language classes might display cuisine or clothing from different cultures. Social studies students might show before-and-after images to see changes in historical sites, or compare types of housing when studying socio-economic differences throughout your city.

✦ **Connect.** Take portraits of members of your school community and interview them about how they relate to a topic in your curriculum, such as their favorite book or food, their reaction to a current event, or what their goals and dreams are for the future.

## Visual Anthropology Project: Humans of Your School

Inspired by the Humans of New York blog by Brandon Stanton, students meet members of their community, have a conversation with them, and take their portrait. Publish a photograph and a summary of the conversation on a social media channel, website, or digital book.

Choose subjects for this project based on your curricular goals, such as an author or poet for an ELA class, an activist for a social studies project, or an engineer for math and science.

# Audio Story Projects
## Oral History Project

Oral history projects help students understand the human dimension of our curriculum by interviewing someone who has experienced it. The interviews at the center of this project allow students to better understand the role of experts and how testimony creates a more complete, nuanced picture of a topic.

Use oral history projects to:

+ interview an expert

+ hear testimony from witnesses and stakeholders

+ develop interview and public speaking skills

+ determine the credibility of sources

+ build foundational skills needed for podcast and documentary projects

Audio allows us to collect nonverbal information, such as emotion, tone of voice, accents, irony, and sarcasm—important social cues that we use all the time to convey information to those around us.

# What's It Take?

**Gear:** Phone or tablet with microphone. Audio recording app, such as Voice Memo. Audio editing app, such as GarageBand or Soundtrap.

**Optional:** External microphone, video camera, video conferencing app like Zoom (to record remote interviews)

**Time to complete this project:** A few minutes to a few hours

**Other considerations:** Make time to research the topic and find sources for interviews, write questions, and review/analyze interview responses.

| BEGINNER ORAL HISTORY IDEAS | ADVANCED ORAL HISTORY IDEAS |
|---|---|
| Interview a friend or family member about an event or time period | Interview an expert or historian |
| Interview a single stakeholder or expert | Interview multiple stakeholders or experts |
| Publish raw interview recordings | Edit interviews for time and clarity. Add music or voiceover |

**FIGURE 12.2** *Listen up: Oral history projects can begin with simpler skill-building stories, then become more complex when students are ready.*

## HOW TO SELECT SOURCES FOR INTERVIEWS

Because oral history projects emphasize the interview—a one-on-one conversation with a stakeholder or expert—it's important for the success and validity of this project to select the right people to be interviewed. Here are some considerations students should think about when choosing interviewees. These same criteria should be used for podcasts and documentary stories:

✦ **Relevance.** To what extent has this person been affected by, or has some responsibility for, the topic? Firsthand experience (a primary source) is best.

✦ **Knowledge.** How knowledgeable are they about this topic (an expert, as a witness, etc.)? Is this the first or only time they've experienced this, or have they dealt with it over a long period?

✦ **Bias.** Why would this person agree to share their story with you? What's at stake for them, and how might they benefit from sharing their perspective? Do they have an agenda or relationship with an untrustworthy organization or group? Do they just want attention?

## STEPS FOR CREATING AN ORAL HISTORY PROJECT

1. Research the topic and find people to interview.

   a. Write better interview questions and have a more dynamic conversation by becoming knowledgeable about the topic and source. It also earns the storyteller credibility and trust from your source.

   b. Verify that your source is credible and knowledgeable about the topic.

   c. Make an effort to interview people from diverse backgrounds, experiences, and geographical regions, not just friends or family.

2. Write interview questions. Create a list of questions to generate responses that are factual (explanation, definitions, clarifications) and also personal reactions and expert opinions (to provide context and help connect the dots). Interview questions should be:

   a. **Specific.** Each question should ask one thing (don't ask for multiple ideas in one question). Know what you're trying to find out.

   b. **Open-ended.** Write questions that can't be answered with "yes" or "no."

   c. **Personal.** Questions should elicit a colorful response that only this source could say.

   d. **Organized.** Ask questions in a logical order.

3. Record the interview.

   a. Record interviews using audio or video. Audio is easily recorded with built-in apps on smartphones and tablets, and video can be recorded with phones and tablets with cameras, video conferencing apps, or standalone video cameras. If video will be used in the final story (like a documentary or explainer video, for example), be sure to light and compose the shot well.

   b. If the final publication format is text, use transcription apps to convert the audio file to text.

# Get Good Sound

The central element of interviews is audio. You need high-quality recordings and clarity of responses to understand the information you're collecting. Here are some quick tips for recording clear, high-quality audio:

✦ use an external microphone whenever possible

✦ get close to the source of sound

✦ avoid noisy locations like busy streets or classrooms

✦ choose interview locations that have soft surfaces like carpeting and upholstered furniture to minimize echo

*Find out more about how to produce podcasts and video interviews using resources listed in appendix A.*

# Podcast

Podcasts have soared in popularity because they are relatively easy to create, and the audience only needs to listen—not read or watch video—which means this kind of story can be experienced while doing other tasks like commuting, cleaning house, or exercising. Use podcasts with students to build on the research and interview techniques developed in the oral history project, and to develop new skills like writing, story structure, and audio editing. Think of podcasts as the less complicated cousin to video documentaries, making it a great step as students move toward that story project.

Where the oral history project often focuses on a single interview or perspective, podcasts allow students to craft a complete picture of a topic by connecting dots and providing context with background information. Podcasts also let students develop a personality and voice for themselves

# What's It Take?

**Gear:** Audio recording apps, audio editing apps.

**Optional:** External microphones for recording high-quality audio. Podcast streaming service account for publishing globally.

**Time to complete this project:** A few hours to a few weeks

**Other considerations:** Depending on the complexity of the project, students will need time to research the topic, schedule interviews with experts or stakeholders, record audio (outside the classroom), and edit their media.

and their show. For podcasts, the inclusion of music, multiple interviews, natural sound, voice-over script, and audio editing opens exciting possibilities for storytelling techniques and audience engagement.

Use podcast story projects to:

✦ develop research and writing skills

✦ practice public speaking

✦ develop interview skills

✦ learn audio editing techniques

✦ build foundational skills for more complex projects like video documentaries

Podcasts come in a variety of genres—from society and culture, to sports, to investigative journalism—making them an easy fit for any classroom, so choose the ones you feel work best for your pedagogical goals or let students surprise you!

## STEPS FOR CREATING A PODCAST STORY PROJECT

Building on the research and interview steps from the oral history project, podcasts may include these additional steps:

1. Record natural sound (optional)

   These are the sounds of a place, people, performance, or other sounds related to the topic and ideas brought up during the interview. This is an important piece of the podcast as it provides audio evidence, helps the audience feel like they are in a specific space, or develops mood, tension, or dramatic suspense.

2. Add music

   Set the tone of a podcast or add humor or drama by adding music under interviews and voiceover or between segments as a transitional element to new topics within an episode. Be sure to use royalty-free music.

3. Edit

   In this phase, students can trim interviews down to only the essential responses, add voiceover for clarification or explanation, and organize information and story elements.

4. Create a show logo

   A graphic logo helps the audience find and recognize podcast stories and is required by streaming services. These are easily created with free online social graphic services, or your favorite art and design app.

| BEGINNER PODCAST IDEAS | ADVANCED PODCAST IDEAS |
|---|---|
| Interview a single stakeholder or witness | Host a panel discussion with multiple stakeholders |
| Record panel discussions live and publish the raw recording | Edit for length and clarity, adding music or voiceover |
| Use genres like commentary or talk show/ interview | Use complex genres like true crime or documentary |

**FIGURE 12.3  Level Up:** *Small adjustments make for more challenging assignments.*

# Avoiding False Equivalencies in Interviews

With recent political and social conflicts, and the exploitation of media platforms to propagate misinformation and disinformation, journalists and social scientists have begun to reexamine their methodology when it comes to objectively gathering qualitative data. No longer do they give equal time to people and organizations with extremist views or when those views are demonstrably false. "Fairness" and "objectivity" are not equations to be balanced by including diametrically opposed extreme (inaccurate) views. That doesn't provide clarity or help us draw conclusions, but only reinforces our pre-existing views, and it doesn't add anything new to the audience's understanding of a topic. Instead of being "fair" to the sources we interview or the sides of an issue they represent, we should instead emphasize fairness to the truth and to one's audience.

This means students need to take time to research and vet their interview sources and to be active, critical listeners during and after the interview. It also means checking one's own biases to see how each of us might interpret statements differently or cause us to choose sources we already agree with or whose ideas make us comfortable. It's also a great reason to develop common standards and guidelines for your class in advance (see chapter 6) to help students make good decisions in times when there is disagreement about or emotional reaction to content in interviews.

## Video Documentary

### What's a Doc?

*The only thing that changes people is storytelling.*
—Ken Burns

Documentaries are one of the most moving and impactful types of storytelling, combining the visual evidence from photography projects, the testimony and expert opinion elements from podcasts, and the context and explanation aspects of explainer videos. They can even be used creatively as a form of personal expression. Unlike journalism, which privileges objectivity, documentaries

## What's It Take?

**Gear:** Video camera, video editing software

**Optional:** Tripod, external microphone, video conferencing app such as Zoom (to record remote interviews)

**Time to complete this project:** A few days to a few weeks or more

**Other considerations:** Allow time to research the topic, find sources for interviews, and record B-roll. Make time for writing interview questions; reviewing/analyzing interview responses; editing footage; and writing and recording a voiceover.

are more like an expository or persuasive essay you might write in a language or social studies class.

At their most fundamental, documentaries are defined as video stories based in the historical world, and they can range the spectrum from highly objective (observational or interactive styles) to highly subjective (personal essay style), making documentaries suitable projects for arts, language, music, and theater arts as much as they are for science or social studies. The workflow and project templates I present here are designed for the interactive documentary style, but like any story project, the fun, creativity, and impact of documentaries are limited only by one's imagination. Find more examples and resources about documentaries online in the Digital Resources.

After teaching cinematic arts for 25 years, I've found documentary projects turn out to be more successful (higher quality, lower stress) if students have already developed some foundational storytelling skills, such as writing, story structure, photography, interviewing, and video editing, usually through their work on less demanding story projects like podcasts or explainer videos. That's because the introduction of video as the primary medium introduces complexities like composition, lighting, camera movement, and the need to record a lot of footage for visual evidence (called B-roll). Stakeholders may also be more reluctant to be recorded on video (as opposed to audio-only in podcasts, for example), making the video footage more challenging for students to create.

# When and How to Use Documentaries

After working with students of all grade levels, I've found these practices to be helpful when teaching documentary filmmaking:

+ **Use documentaries as a replacement for exams or final essays.** Use docs as a long-term, summative project that is completed at the end of a unit or semester using research and knowledge developed during that time.

+ **Scaffold skills first.** Before you ask your students to make a documentary, have them create podcasts and explainer videos to build foundational skills.

+ **Plan ahead.** Introduce the project at the start of your unit so students can document as they learn. If a specific event or phenomenon happens only once, they need to be prepared to record it.

+ **Shoot first, write voiceover later.** Docs should never be illustrated essays, where students write a traditional essay, record themselves reading it, and then tack on video footage. Remember, documentaries are a type of inquiry that use cameras and microphones to collect samples and evidence, like scientists doing fieldwork. While it's helpful to have a story outline in advance, I've found it's best to begin by recording video footage and interviews, which are the core evidence and facts of the story, then write the voiceover script in response to that evidence.

- **Less is more.** Long projects take a lot of effort and can be difficult to produce. Make it easy on your students and their audience by keeping docs to two to five minutes in length, and no more than five to ten minutes in length for experienced students.
- **Serialize complex topics.** Instead of one giant 30-minute documentary, consider having students create micro-documentaries of one to three minutes each throughout your inquiry-based unit. Post these story installments as chapters in a digital book or on your social media channel.

## Steps for Creating a Documentary Project

Documentaries use the same workflow as other story projects like explainer videos and oral history projects, so model your workflow on those already discussed:

1. Research the topic
2. Develop a focus statement
3. Identify sources to be interviewed (stakeholders, experts, witnesses, etc.)
4. Develop interview questions and record interviews (with video)
5. Create a story outline and script

In addition to these steps, students will need to include two additional parts of the process: recording B-roll and editing the footage and other media together.

### B-ROLL

This is video footage that is recorded to illustrate facts and information and should help transport the audience to the places discussed in the doc. While it is often used as visual evidence to support a fact or statement by an interviewee, B-roll can also be used to refute claims made by those who make false or uninformed statements.

### EDITING

This is the final step of the project, in which students assemble and organize all their story media. It's also an opportunity to fine-tune the story and ensure clarity with the selection of B-roll. This is the most time-consuming phase of making the documentary, and you should expect it to take two to three times longer than the initial recording of footage.

Review and revise documentaries to fine-tune, check for accuracy, or add new footage or information. Publish videos on a website, social media channel, or embed them into a digital book. Find more resources for producing documentaries in appendix A.

# Privacy, Trust, and the Intruding Video Camera

In the same way a thermometer changes the temperature of a substance that it's measuring, video cameras can change how people act or respond while recording interviews or B-roll. Cameras can make some people nervous or want to perform, instead of acting naturally.

Other people are reluctant to be interviewed on camera or even be recorded as part of the background for B-roll. There are many potential reasons for this, including mistrust of journalists or concern for one's appearance or privacy. Student storytellers should always be transparent about their intentions and ask permission before recording footage. See resources for ethical storytelling in appendix B.

**FIGURE 12.4** *Storytelling as research: Students conduct qualitative reseach by interviewing experts and stakeholders, and recording visual evidence for documentaries, all while learning observation and interpersonal skills, and how to write good questions.*

# CHAPTER 13
# STORYTELLING FOR CREATIVITY AND DESIGN

As my college English professor once said, "There is no such thing as 'creative writing'—ALL writing is creative." While every story project in this book uses creativity in every definition of the word (from developing story ideas, to composition, to color and font choices), this chapter covers story projects that embrace creativity wholeheartedly in their execution as well as their concept. But these projects aren't just for art students—they inject passion and fun into what can often be dry subject matter and help students use both sides of their brains when learning your curriculum.

## Illustrations

Pictorial storytelling is one of the oldest and most profound forms of communicating ideas, instructions, relationships, and emotions—sometimes all at once. Images can be simultaneously more specific than words and also more abstract (think symbols and emojis, abstract paintings, and memes). This makes illustrations fertile ground for learning, as they open up so many great opportunities for conversations with students around clarity and specificity, interpretation, cultural bias, and complex curricular content, like literary devices such as irony and metaphor.

Educators often consider illustrations a quaint form of personal expression, completed after "serious" work is finished, either as a reward or as a flourish that gives color to a drab report. But when handled properly, illustration projects provide experiences that develop critical thinking skills, activate abstract thought, and are an important way for student storytellers to reach a broad contemporary audience.

## Cover Art and Editorial Illustrations

As we discussed in chapter 2, illustrations are a great way to integrate art and design with other curriculum, by designing an image that relates to, comments on, or reflects the themes of an existing work, such as a novel, film, news article, historical event, or student-produced story. Book and album covers typically reflect the contents of a creative work, whereas editorial illustrations typically accompany a news, science, or cultural article.

### CREATING EDITORIAL ILLUSTRATIONS

This project can be introduced after students have studied or created a story, or better yet, introduced at the start of the unit so that students can be thinking about the illustration and looking for details to include in their project as they research, read, and experience the source material.

# What's It Take?

**Gear:** Apps dedicated to creating illustrations, such as drawing apps, photo collage tools, or whiteboard or presentation apps like Keynote.

**Time to complete this project:** A few hours to a few days

✦ Understand the source material. Determine the main themes, concepts, or takeaways of the source material, people involved, materials, objects, or tools related to the story, etc. These will be used in the next steps.

✦ Develop the concept. Come up with a plan for the look or design of the illustration. Will it be literal and show specific people/objects/places from the topic, or be metaphorical or symbolic? Write a description and/or sketch what the final

| DIFFICULTY LEVEL | ILLUSTRATION PROJECT |
|---|---|
| Easy | **Album Cover** <br> Have students choose an existing album to design a cover for, using topics, themes, and music genres as inspiration for their design. |
| Moderate | **Book Cover or Podcast Cover Art** <br> Let students design a cover for a book they've read or created from your curriculum. Or have students design a podcast cover for their own series or a new one for an existing show. |
| Advanced | **Editorial Illustration** <br> Create an illustration based on concepts from a research article, or for student stories. Design with the intent of publishing them within a story project like a book, website, or as a social media post. |

**FIGURE 13.1  Art of learning:** *Illustrations require high level thinking to create metaphors, irony, and social commentary.*

illustration will look like and how the concept explores the ideas within the source material.

✦ Collect media. If creating a collage, collect or create images used in the final illustration.

If creating a drawing or painting, practice illustration techniques.

✦ Make the illustration. Use your favorite digital tools or analog equivalents.

*FIGURE 13.2* *Editorial illustrations like these made by my students Maddox Chen (top), Luke Rytz (bottom left), and Ava Aguero (bottom right) use irony, humor, and critical thinking to help audiences think about topics in new ways. Maddox's illustration was published in the* New York Times *as part of a feature on teens during the COVID pandemic.*

## Memes

A common type of story on social media is the meme, which is an image, typically of a person or situation, with text added on top as a form of comedic commentary. While seemingly a recent phenomenon in the social media age, its roots extend back hundreds—some say thousands—of years and include respected forms of storytelling like political cartoons.

Use memes to quickly create a powerful message using a single image and open discussions around humor (what makes something humorous, what is appropriate and what might not be), cultural and political references, co-opting images and social messaging, and our responsibility as authors when posting content on social media. It's also a great way to introduce high-level concepts like irony and sarcasm.

### THE PROCESS FOR CREATING MEMES

Because of its small scale and minimal technical requirements, this project has a lot of flexibility in terms of when you can use it. The hardest part is coming up with the idea. Use memes to introduce a concept or kick off a unit by tapping into student perceptions or misperceptions of a topic, or at the end of a unit have students create memes based on their new knowledge.

✦ Introduce and define memes by discussing contemporary and historical examples.

✦ Discuss the concepts of irony, sarcasm, contradictions, and humor.

## What's It Take?

**Gear:** Any app that lets you add text to an image, such as photo apps with markup tools that come pre-installed on student devices.

**Time to complete this project:** A few minutes to a few hours

**Other considerations:** Factor in time to introduce concepts of memes, including humor and historical examples, and time to create and revise the image/text. Think about when and where to publish the memes, such as a class social media channel, or included as part of a larger story, such as a digital book or website.

✦ Have students choose a subject for their meme, either from research related to curriculum or discovered during the production of a larger story project. This is particularly fruitful when addressing misperceptions or misunderstandings of a topic.

✦ Find or create an image, typically a photograph.

✦ Write several options for the meme text, then choose the best one.

✦ Create the meme, share, and publish.

# Graphic Novels

Graphic novels have evolved a lot since the early days of superhero comics and are now a respected form of nonfiction narrative that includes sub-genres like biography, memoir, and documentary. Graphic novels like *Persepolis* have won international acclaim, and *Maus* was the first graphic novel to receive the Pulitzer Prize.

The advantage of graphic novels is that, unlike video or animations, they have the permanence of static images—audiences can take their time to look at and process the images and accompanying text. It's easy to tell stories that make comparisons, show the steps of a process and stages of events, or even show multiple times or places on the same page. Unlike editorial illustrations or memes, graphic novels are comprised of multiple images—perhaps as few as two or three panels, or as many as a complete book—to explain complex ideas or show progress or change over time.

Use graphic novels to:

✦ describe, define, or explain a concept in the same way you might use infographics or explainer videos

✦ tell stories using a combination of multiple illustrations and text in sequence

✦ show abstract concepts that are difficult or impossible to record with photos or video, such as historical figures and events; scientific concepts like evolution; application of mathematical formulas to real-world examples; or biographies of artists and authors

✦ show multiple ideas, concepts, and times at once, to create comparisons or show contrasts

# What's It Take?

**Gear:** Apps dedicated to creating illustrations. This might include traditional drawing/painting apps or non-traditional workarounds like whiteboard apps or presentation software. Many digital book apps and online design services have comic book templates to get you started.

**Time to complete this project:** A few hours to a few days or weeks

**Other considerations:** Creating illustrations can take much longer than photographs or video, so allow time for students to create images this way.

## Steps of the Process for Creating Graphic Novels

Developing a graphic novel begins with writing a story outline or script, and then creating the illustrations and/or page layout. Use a process similar to the one for an explainer video or editorial illustration, by determining the images that best convey the ideas to the audience, then deciding what media might be needed to create the images.

Illustrations don't have to be hand-drawn or painted. Students can also use template-based apps, photo illustrations, or collage techniques. Consider working in small teams to collaborate on a graphic novel, such as having each student be responsible for one section or chapter of a larger book, or perhaps even having students specialize in one area of the creative process, such as having some students write the script while others create the illustrations. As always, start small (like a two- or three-panel story), then assign more ambitious projects once students have more experience.

+ Introduce the graphic novel medium, using exemplars.

+ Develop a story by creating a page-by-page or panel-by-panel outline as a written description only (similar to the process used for explainer videos).

+ Create or gather media needed to create the illustrations.

+ Create the illustrations.

+ Add text, titles, and other elements needed to explain concepts not immediately clear in the images.

+ Publish as a digital book, on a website, or as panels of a social media post.

# Animation

Cartoons and movies like those created by Pixar are a fun way to tell stories, but animation is also a powerful form of storytelling used by scientists, journalists, and others to explain complex or abstract concepts, especially when we can't document them with photos or video. Think of how animated sequences are used by NASA to explain satellite and planetary exploration missions or how meteorologists show weather patterns. If you're a child of the '70s like me, you probably remember *Schoolhouse Rock!*, the Saturday morning cartoons that used animation to teach subjects like U.S. civics in just a few minutes. I like to think of animation as a hybrid of graphic novels, editorial illustrations, and explainer videos, drawing on the strengths of each medium, such as illustration, movement, text, and voiceover to help explain complex ideas or topics.

| DIFFICULTY LEVEL | GRAPHIC NOVEL PROJECT |
|---|---|
| Easy | Two- to Three-Panel Story |
| | Two panels are great for compare/contrast situations. Or use three panels to introduce the beginning/middle/end three-act story structure, and how to design a complete story economically. |
| Moderate | Poster Infographic |
| | Create a single-page poster or infographic using multiple panels that can be printed or shared on a website. |
| Advanced | Graphic Novel |
| | Create a multi-page story, published as a digital book or pages of a website. Level up by making this a collaborative story or by adding video, GIFs, or animations instead of static illustrations alone. |

**FIGURE 13.3** *Panel discussion: Combine images and text to create unique narrative structures.*

# What's It Take?

**Gear:** Apps dedicated to creating animation, or presentation software such as Keynote

**Time to complete this project:** A few hours to a few days or weeks

**Other considerations:** Factor in time to teach basic animation techniques, and for students to create or collect media needed for the animations like maps, photos, and other objects.

Traditional animation uses a stop-motion technique that requires a unique illustration or position of an object for each frame of video. Fortunately, there are many ways to create animated stories that are faster and less complicated.

There are many apps that help students create animations easily and quickly—even a transition between slides in a presentation app like Keynote can create a powerful animation. Export animated stories as videos to include in explainer videos, documentaries, websites, social media posts, or digital books.

Use animation:

+ in the same way you might use video to create movement or show change. Try animating data visualizations to show changes over time; animate maps, diagrams, or passages of text to direct the audience's attention to a specific area

+ in the same way you might use explainer videos to describe, define, or explain a concept

+ when it is difficult or impossible to record photos or video of the topic, such as scientific principles like gravity or magnetism; topics that span a long period of time, such as erosion, change of borders, or migration patterns; discussing historical events or figures; or explaining abstract concepts like psychological conditions, political and demographic shifts, or musical and literary concepts like rhythm and pacing

+ as an opportunity to integrate visual art into your curriculum

## Steps of the Process for Creating Animated Stories

Follow the same steps you would for creating an explainer video, starting with a voiceover script and scene-by-scene or slide-by-slide shot list. Then record and publish the story.

1.  Introduce animation as a way to explain ideas, using exemplars

2.  Write a script and shot list or slide outline

3.  Design slides or animation frames (if using an animation app)

4.  Record and export the animation

5.  Use video editing tools to add voiceover, sound effects, music, titles, or other elements if desired

6.  Publish the animation as a social media post, or include in an explainer video, documentary, website, or digital book.

| DIFFICULTY LEVEL | ANIMATION PROJECT |
| --- | --- |
| Easy | Data Visualization |
| | Many apps allow students to create animated graphs and charts by including multiple data sets to show change over time, location, or demographics. |
| Moderate | Animated GIF |
| | These short, looping videos are a great way to show a process or timeline in just a few seconds. Use apps that create .gif files or export animations from presentation software. |
| Advanced | Animated Stories |
| | Use presentation apps like Keynote to create longer, more complex animation sequences by using transitions between slides, or animating objects within a slide. |

**FIGURE 13.4  E-motion:** *Animation isn't just for cartoons. Use it when you need to show movement and change, to describe abstract concepts, or phenomena you can't record with video or photography..*

# CHAPTER 14
# ADVOCACY: STORY PROJECTS THAT INSPIRE ACTION

*We must always take sides. Neutrality helps the oppressor, never the victim. Silence encourages the tormentor, never the tormented.*

**—Elie Wiesel**

Storytelling is about much more than acquiring skills or regurgitating facts. It is about helping students learn how they might use these skills and knowledge to advocate for positive social change. Making a difference is part of National Geographic Education's Explorer Mindset, and it's why media literacy is defined as not only being able to decode digital messages but to use these skills to take action (NAMLE, 2020). In my friend Dr. Jennifer Williams's book, *Teach Boldly*, she outlines why and how we can empower students to improve the world around us.

While we can use storytelling projects for skill building and assessment of existing curriculum, I would argue that the highest-level, most effective learning experiences are those that have purpose beyond merely grading. This is what we mean when we say we want students to be empowered: to invite and trust them to use the knowledge and skills they learn in our classrooms to make a positive impact on the world. Sometimes this means sharing ideas objectively, like journalists or scientists. Other times it means taking a stand and using ethical decision-making to become community leaders through the creation and publishing of stories that matter. These kinds of stories help students evolve from passive learners into active ones, and, by extension, provide a way for students to evolve from being passive bystanders into active citizens.

While students can use any of the projects in this book to advocate for positive change, those discussed in this section in particular lend themselves to advocacy story projects.

# What Do We Mean by "Advocacy"?

*I am no longer accepting the things I cannot change. I am changing the things I cannot accept.*

**Angela Davis**

Advocacy story projects are those that make the case for a change of mindset, policy, or behavior. Topics of any scale are important, from the personal to the global, and can include issues such as arguing for healthier food in the cafeteria or requesting a stop sign at a busy intersection, to global topics like climate justice or women's rights. This is a great substitute for debates or persuasive essays, because digital stories about these topics often require students to interact with stakeholders, and they have a much larger audience—and therefore more impact—than classroom-bound projects like speeches and reports.

Advocacy is different from arguments that one might have in debates in that it is focused more on positive, collaborative solutions than on developing antagonistic, competitive dichotomies of winners and losers. Advocacy may also be about making space for underrepresented or marginalized people or developing the courage to discuss controversial or uncomfortable topics. Choosing a topic can in itself be a form of advocacy because it says to the audience that a subject is worthy of our attention.

# Fostering an Advocacy Mindset for Storytellers

Like any story project, the most effective advocacy stories are compelling, personal, authentic, and identifiable. Didactic monologues tend to fall flat and become boring. Instead, approach these kinds of projects from a place of humility, where students center listening rather than talking. Audiences don't want to be told what to think and instead respond more positively when stories allow them to make sense of the ideas independently. Interviews with experts and stakeholders for oral history projects and documentaries are a good place to start. Remember, this isn't a rant or an argument unsupported by evidence but an opportunity to use research and critical thinking to address a challenge in the world by offering solutions.

## ADVOCACY THROUGH EMPATHY

Instead of having students turn the camera or microphone on themselves, have them use research methods outlined in chapter 8 to determine what big topic they want to address and to gather evidence they might need to make their case. A great way to do this is by collaborating with or telling the stories of stakeholder groups affected by a topic. Begin with empathy interviews and encourage these stakeholders to appear in the digital story, either as a voice on a podcast, in images of a portrait or photojournalism series, or as an interview in a documentary. This provides authentic, human examples of a topic, which are much more believable and empathetic than a "voice of god" (omniscient narrator) story where student authors preach from an ivory tower.

# Teaching History Backwards

I've always disliked the concept of teaching history chronologically, from the beginning of time until now. Students struggle to see the importance of historical events of even 20 or 30 years ago or how they matter in the contemporary world. Since humans keep making history, social studies teachers often run out of time to do justice to current events that have a direct impact on our students' lives. To address these issues, have students start with current events and create advocacy story projects about a contemporary issue. As part of their research, they must discover the historical, political, and cultural origins of the topic. It's a great way for students to make connections between the past and present and helps them see the value of studying the past.

"Living in fear is not living at all."
- Christopher

*Living in fear, wondering if they will ever have to go back and re-live their past. This constant fear haunts them. Scared to know what will happen to their future and the people who are apart of them.*

**FIGURE 14.1** *This photo essay project by my student Vanessa Lopez focused on the story of undocumented immigrants to the U.S. By hearing the stories of these immigrants, she added a human element that is often missing from political discussions around the topic.*

While the style, method, and techniques students use for advocacy varies by the type of story they use (documentaries are very different from podcasts or data visualizations, for instance), here are some general tips for developing an effective advocacy story project.

✦ Avoid monologues and speeches. Embrace the unique strengths of digital storytelling to create emotion, empathy, and engagement.

✦ In most cases, avoid a "hard sell" approach of bombarding the audience with statistics, especially at the beginning of a story.

✦ Tell a personal anecdote to help the audience be more receptive to the author.

✦ Make a human connection by telling the story of someone affected by the topic, either through interviews or by using visual evidence like photography or video.

✦ Add humor where appropriate. While it can be tricky to pull off, when done well, it can lower the audience's defenses and make them more willing to listen to the ideas being put forth in the story.

# Public Service Announcement

Public service announcements (PSAs) are video advertising campaigns that sell positive social behaviors instead of products. These might include topics like anti-bullying, recycling, seatbelt wearing, and distracted driving awareness. The "Crying Indian" Native American paddling through a polluted creek, and the "This is your brain on drugs" campaigns are famous professional examples. They use a variety of techniques, including emotion, to engage the audience, and have a call to

# What's It Take?

**Gear:** Word processing apps for planning and writing. Video cameras and apps for video editing.

**Time to complete this project:** A few hours to a few days or weeks

**Other considerations:** Factor in time to teach about persuasive writing, sharing examples, writing effective taglines, and discussing concepts like propaganda and misinformation. Allow time for recording and editing video footage.

action that encourages either a change of behavior, change of mindset, or both.

PSAs are a great project because they are short (30 to 60 seconds), can be completed in just a few hours or days, and integrate all the elements of digital storytelling. I use them as a summative assessment in the first semester of my cinematic arts class, and to scaffold longer, more complicated narrative film projects in the second semester.

Use PSAs:

✦ to teach persuasive writing, advertising, and marketing

✦ to introduce the concepts of propaganda and misinformation

✦ as a low-stakes project that takes less time than more complicated video stories like documentaries

✦ as a summative assignment that utilizes all aspects of the storytelling process

✦ to introduce constructive use of social media (if publishing there)

*FIGURE 14.2  This award-winning PSA discussed in chapter 8 was produced by my student Avery Gregory to encourage energy savings to combat climate change. Find a link to the video in the Digital Resources.*

## Steps of the Process for Creating PSAs

PSAs can be created individually, but try teams of two to three students for the best experience. The process is similar to creating an explainer video or mini documentary.

1. Use a story-generating process from chapter 6 to decide what the main topic will be.

2. Narrow down the idea to a specific call to action: a specific action you want the audience to take or a shift of mindset you want them to adopt after watching this story. For example, reducing single-use plastic, exercising more, or seeing the fun of riding bikes to school instead of driving.

3. Create a tagline. This is a clever, memorable phrase that often concludes advertisements like "Got Milk?" and "Just Do It."

4. Write a script using the two-column format in chapter 15, then make a shot list of video clips to record.

5. Shoot the video clips.

6. Edit the video.

7. Publish on a website, digital book, or social media channel.

## Social Impact Graphic

An easier alternative to the PSA is a social impact graphic, a single image or series of images that brings awareness to a topic or advocates for a change of behavior or mindset. It's different from a meme in that its focus is more about encouraging a positive change rather than simply critiquing a social or political concept, although there might be some overlap.

Use social impact graphics for the same reasons you'd use a PSA, and also:

✦ when you have less time or resources but still want an advocacy story project

✦ when you want students to create a project individually

✦ as a low-stakes way to introduce and provide a purpose for graphic design skills

✦ to model productive use of social media (if publishing there)

### Steps of the Social Impact Graphic Process

Creating a social impact graphic is a cross between a PSA and a meme or editorial illustration, so follow the steps of those projects: determine the topic, develop the concept and tagline, create the images, then design the graphic. Like all story projects, allow students time to come up with a few ideas, then workshop them to revise and determine the best one to develop into the final project. It might also be helpful to let students sketch a design as part of the iteration process. Create the final project on your design app of choice, such as presentation software or online social graphics apps.

## More Advocacy Story Project Ideas

Choose any of the story projects to turn into an advocacy story, or try these:

✦ **POV.** A point-of-view story is similar to editorials in newspapers, where the author creates a podcast or explainer video to make their point. This could also be published as a social media story, and audience members can be encouraged to reply with comments.

✦ **Panel discussions.** Choose a topic and invite different stakeholders to share their perspectives and have a conversation with each other. This works great as a podcast or a recorded video conference. Keep it short and share discussion questions with guests in advance.

✦ **Video essay.** A hybrid of a written essay and explainer video, a video essay lets the author meditate on a topic, explaining or interpreting an artwork, piece of literature or film, or a historical event. Video essays are to explainer videos what essays are to journalism stories: more of an analysis/reflection by the author than a strictly objective explanation.

# CHAPTER 15
# WRITING FOR DIGITAL STORYTELLING

Writing is at the heart of every digital story, even if it's not done explicitly with text. If we think of images, video clips, presentation slides, or pages of a book as words, we can arrange them into unique types of sentences or paragraphs that evoke suspense and curiosity, provide context, and create meaning for an audience. The process of writing for digital stories—whether using multimedia, text, or both—is an opportunity to make parallels to other kinds of writing you already do in the classroom. It also provides many benefits for developing stronger writers:

✦ Quick, short stories, which thrive in a digital format, create low-risk opportunities for success and encourage creative and intellectual risk-taking.

✦ Self-selected stories can bring joy and create buy-in for assignments.

✦ Brief digital stories like social media posts and illustrations have the flexibility to address current events and new developments related to your curriculum (e.g., scientific breakthroughs, political events, publishing of new artistic work, etc.)

✦ Stories created on recurring schedules, for example weekly posts for social media, help writers evolve more quickly and track their progress.

Producing digital stories provides many of the same advantages as traditional writing assignments, such as helping students to:

✦ wonder, dream, and ruminate

✦ conduct research

✦ clarify thinking and organize thoughts

✦ express ideas

✦ process difficult personal, social, and political challenges

✦ empathize with an audience and capture their attention

✦ market and publicize a story

This chapter is about how we can use words, images, and sound—individually or together—to develop stories and build an experience that effectively communicates ideas to an audience.

# Writing for Ideation

Keeping a journal is a common activity for creatives, scientists, or anyone tracking and making sense of their life. Use journaling and dream-catching techniques to encourage your students to compile an informal, ongoing collection of ideas, thoughts, quotes, photos, and video and audio clips that can later become the spark of inspiration for story projects. Try a more formal method like Wonder Journals discussed in chapter 6 to foster a mindset of curiosity, observation, and reflection.

The process of writing itself, especially through the creation of multiple drafts, can help students find the story they're looking for and leverage the feedback in workshops to elevate their ideas.

# Writing for Research

Research is an active practice of discovering, reflecting upon, and determining the most surprising, relevant, and meaningful ideas. Using writing as part of research requires high-level critical thinking to determine what matters most in alignment with project goals and class mission statements.

# Annotated Bibliographies

Annotated bibliographies, commonly used in high school and college when creating research papers, are also useful for digital story projects. For each bibliography created in the appropriate format (MLA, APA, Chicago, etc.), students write a two- to three-sentence summary of the key findings in this resource. This not only provides accountability for reading the resource but also helps students determine the most important and relevant data to cite or use when creating stories.

Annotated bibliographies can also be a story in themselves. Create social graphics related to research article findings or use this information later when promoting and marketing a larger story based on this research. Pulling surprising statistics or quotes from research documents is a great way to do so.

Shah, P. E., Weeks, H. M., Richards, B., & Kaciroti, N. (2018). Early childhood curiosity and kindergarten reading and math academic achievement. Pediatric Research, 84(3), 380–386. https://doi.org/10.1038/s41390-018-0039-3

In a study of kindergarteners, kids with greater curiosity perform better in reading and math. The effect is especially pronounced with low SES children. Researchers say these findings about curiosity should be emphasized in schools to improve student academic performance.

**CURIOSITY**
increases academic achievement by

**20%**
reading

**11%**
math

And is even more effective for low SES students

SOURCE: Pediatric Research, April 2018

**FIGURE 15.1** *In this example of an annotated bibliography, a student has summarized the key findings and determined the most important ideas in this article. This info is useful for background knowledge as they produce explainer videos, documentaries, or digital books, but can also be a story in itself. The second image is a graphic using information from the same article, but instead of burying the findings in a bibliography, the student created a story to share the findings of this article with a wider audience via social media.*

## Interview Questions

Developing interview questions is a wonderful learning experience because it is at once an act of research, a way to find mental clarity, and a process for developing interpersonal skills and empathy. Students must focus their ideas to compose effective questions that make sense to others, provide specificity, and evoke helpful responses. Understanding each interviewee helps students craft questions tailored to that source's unique knowledge, experience, and personality.

In addition to the tips outlined in chapter 6, try these advanced techniques for writing good interview questions.

✦ **Be humble.** Ask sources to explain terms, concepts, or events. This honors the source's experience and can also ensure accuracy for the storyteller.

✦ **Clarify.** Help answer lingering questions student authors might have about a topic or facts from their research. Try phrases like "What does this mean?" and "Help me understand . . ."

◆ **Write questions exactly as you'll say them, instead of using bullet points.** This helps clarify thinking in advance and avoids forgetting the point of the question—especially when students get nervous during the interview.

◆ **Write questions as a prompt.** This helps create a conversation rather than an interrogation. Present the interviewee with a situation, fact, or statement, then have them respond to it. Follow the prompt with phrases like: "How do you explain that?" "What would you say to someone who feels that way?" or "How does that make you feel?" or "How is your experience different from that?"

◆ **End interviews by letting the source add their perspective to fill gaps in student questioning and make them feel respected.** Try questions like "What am I missing?" and "Is there anything else you'd like to share about this topic?"

Students can create draft questions, and then ask for feedback from peers or the teacher. Make revisions accordingly before recording the interview.

| QUESTION | PROBLEM | BETTER QUESTION |
|---|---|---|
| Is it a good idea to take public transportation? | Avoid asking "yes" or "no" questions to elicit more detailed responses. | What are some of the benefits of taking public transportation? Or: What advice would you give to people who are reluctant to use public transportation? |
| Does your novel have more than one source of inspiration, and if so, how did you decide what to focus on? | Combining multiple questions confuses the interviewee. Do your research and decide what specific fact you're looking for, then write that as a question. | I've read that you had multiple sources of inspiration for your novel. How did you choose your final themes? Or: Of all your life experiences, why choose *this* for your novel's theme? |
| Of the many things that affect player performance on the field, which would you personally say people should know about? | Vague and confusing. Know what facts you're looking for and write questions that elicit those responses. | What is your biggest concern for player safety right now? Or: What are healthy dietary choices athletes can make to improve their performance? |

**FIGURE 15.2 Ask better questions:** *Knowing what questions to ask is key to deeper understanding and creating an effective story.*

# Interview Question Workshop

Help students develop interview questions with a low-stakes question writing lab.

✦ Have students interview each other about a topic of choice or a current event.

✦ Write questions to interview an author or historical figure from your curriculum.

✦ Practice writing questions to elicit facts and others that spark personal reactions.

✦ Discuss the questions in small groups, share the most intriguing and thought-provoking questions with the rest of the class, and talk about what made them so effective. Give feedback on question effectiveness, clarity, and sequence, then make revisions.

## Empathy Interviews: Summarize and Clarify Thinking

This essential phase of research discussed in chapter 6 is not only a chance to gather ideas and information but also an opportunity for students to evaluate these ideas to determine the most important information and find the direction of their project. Once students have conducted their interviews, the next step is to review their notes or recordings to understand ideas discussed and evaluate the conversation. Create written summaries using prompts like:

✦ What new perspectives, information, and ideas did you hear?

✦ What surprised you?

✦ Describe stories or anecdotes shared in the interview that resonated with you—if they are interesting to you, they're probably interesting to the audience

✦ What part of the conversation was the source particularly passionate about?

✦ What new questions do you have about the topic as a result of your interview?

# Scripts for Digital Storytelling

Scripts are both the skeleton and flesh of a story, providing an organizational role, a checklist for production, and the detailed finishing touches. Writing scripts is an exercise in abstract and critical thinking because it requires students to figure out how to organize a story, determine what information is most important, and choose the exact words and phrasing (including metaphors and analogies) for how to best explain concepts and ideas.

Writing scripts for nonfiction stories can often be a chicken and egg situation. You don't always know what to write until you've gathered all your information from interviews and recordings, but you also don't know what questions to ask or footage to record unless you have an outline for your story. This often means—especially for video stories and podcasts—that students might continue to revise the script and story structure while researching, shooting, and editing.

# Scripts for Video Stories

Scripts are formatted to provide consistency from project to project—for example, to plan for production by knowing what shots to record or questions to ask. They also help make the editing phase easier by aligning images and interview soundbites in the sequence outlined in the script.

*FIGURE 15.3 Use a word processing app to create a two-column script for video PSAs. One column has a description of video images, and the other has the corresponding audio, like dialogue/voice-over, music, or sound effects. For explainer videos, describe the content of slides in the "Video" column, and the voice over script in the "Audio" column.*

**PSA TITLE:** "Thrifty"  **Target audience:** Teens in the U.S.  **Technique:** Humor, self-image

| VIDEO | AUDIO |
|---|---|
| Young girl (Lily) looks at a pile of clothes switching to a close up at the camera | **Lily:** "Ugh all of these old clothes I have to throw away, but you know what that means shopping!" |
| Mid shot of Lily throwing some of the clothes in the air | **Music:** light happy music |
| Camera montage clips to a extreme close up on her boyfriends (Jake) eyes lit up with an idea | **SFX:** suspenseful, consequential sounds |
| Close up on Jake speaking to Lily/Camera | **Jake** (VO): "What was I told… the environment. Thrifting?.. That's it!…" |
| Over head shot → Lily looks up at camera drops her clothes and switches to a medium shot of her speaking to Lily | **Jake:** "Babe, you can't throw those away. I found out the Fashion Industry causes 10% of carbon emission which is totally like affecting our atmosphere " |
| Close up on Jake shaking his head speaking to camera | **Lily** : "Gasps.. What do I do then?!" **SFX:** suspenseful sounds become louder |
| Montage clips in a fast pace of them packing the clothes and driving/heading to the thrift store | **Jake:** "Pack your clothes we're heading to the thrift store" |
| Wide shot of them facing/looking up at  the thrift store | **Music** : fun cheerful upbeat song |
| Medium shot of Lily's face still confused and grossed out | **Lily** "I thought thrift stores were for like the homeless?" |
| Wide shot of the couple and store behind them Jake has hands on her reassuring her | **Jake:** "What no, besides I got my jacket here and you love it?" |
| Extreme close up on Lily's eyes starring switch to close up on his jacket | **Lily:** "Oh really… okay!" |
| **Montage sequence** (fast forward speed) of Lily and Jake returning their clothes and shopping in the thrift store: trying on clothes, emerging from changing rooms in a variety of outfits that are funny or don't match, having fun and joking with one another, then finally emerging from the changing room with a stylish outfit. | **Music:** Cheerful fun music continues |
| They emerge from the store to receive admiring looks from passersby. | **ANNCR:** "Look good while saving money AND the environment…'" |
| TITLE CARD: Reduce, reuse… Refashion | **ANNCR:** "Reduce, reuse, refashion" |

These two-column scripts are used for PSAs, documentaries, and explainer videos. One column is a description of video or images, and the other column has the associated audio, which creates clarity on which story elements go together.

## Scripts for Podcasts

Since podcasts have no visual component, these scripts only include voiceover and interview questions. Scripts are slightly different, depending on how many hosts you have, but the basic structure looks something like this:

+ **Introduction.** A brief summary to let the audience know what this episode is about. It should be catchy, to intrigue the audience and get them to listen. Include the podcast tagline, introduce the host, and even use clips from interviews.

+ **Guest intro.** If interviewing a guest, share their bio to let the audience know who they are, what their background is, and what unique and important insights they'll provide.

+ **Interview questions.** If this is an interview-style podcast, write questions here in the order they'll be asked.

+ **Outro.** Like a concluding paragraph in an essay, this is a summary of takeaways, reflections, and a recap of the episode. It's a good place to thank your guests, introduce your next episode, and point people to where they can contact you or find more information about the episode topic.

## Writing a Voiceover

Adding a narrator's voiceover to video images is a common technique used by documentarians and broadcast journalists to explain concepts, provide context, introduce/transition topics, or describe what cannot immediately be seen. Use this technique for video stories and podcasts.

Tips for writing and recording voiceover (VO) scripts:

+ Use a two-column script format with visuals on one side and the corresponding VO script on the other.

+ Write VOs after video clips and interviews have been recorded so that the script can respond to and play off soundbites (quotes from interviews) and B-roll.

+ Say it, show it: If you say something in your VO, you must also show it with B-roll or a graphic/animation. It provides visual evidence to verify a statement and provides more clarity than words alone.

+ Use the writing style appropriate for digital stories. (See below.)

+ Record in a quiet space, with soft surfaces like upholstered furniture or carpet to minimize echo.

+ Performing a VO requires energy and enthusiasm. Speak as if this is the most important story your audience needs to hear right now.

+ Enunciate clearly. Rehearse and make sure you know how to pronounce proper nouns and acronyms. Record multiple times to get it right.

# How to Sound Like a Real Person

Writing for digital stories is very different from traditional academic or journalistic writing in both content and style. Digital stories function differently, and the audience interacts with them in dynamic ways, so writing for them is more economical and direct. Unlike newspapers or websites, the audience can't glance back to reread a paragraph of text in a podcast or video story—it's got to be clear on the first pass.

Voiceover scripts are less formal, more personable, and typically structured with the subject at the start of sentences and paragraphs.

Here are some tips on writing style for voiceovers:

✦ Write conversationally, as if you were explaining this topic to a friend or your mother, including using the first person.

✦ Avoid flowery language.

✦ Use contractions, phrases, and short sentences rather than long sentences and paragraphs. Mimic real-life conversation techniques.

✦ Round off complex numbers. $1,475,728, for example, should be written as "About one point five million dollars."

✦ Write for the ear: repeat, summarize, and restate throughout the script. Because VO words are invisible to the audience, it can be helpful to repeat yourself periodically to provide clarity.

✦ Use the active voice and write in the present or future tense.

# Writing for Context

Writing can be used effectively to complement multimedia stories, and it is a good way to transition from traditional writing assignments to those that rely more heavily on multimedia. Including text side by side with other media in digital books, blogs, websites, or social media posts helps provide background information that isn't immediately clear in those story formats, enhances the audience experience, and helps a multimedia story become more easily searchable online. Use the strengths of text to:

✦ create episode descriptions (brief summaries) for podcasts and videos

✦ include statistics or facts that are hard to understand in audio or video

✦ facilitate audience interaction by adding links to resources

Use writing within student stories to:

✦ practice more traditional writing within the context of a dynamic multimedia one

✦ have students explain what they learned when creating a multimedia story

✦ provide transparency about the storytelling process (research, challenges, technical steps, etc.)

✦ market their story by writing blurbs (short, catchy synopses) used when publishing digital books or submitting projects to competitions

# Organizing Thoughts: How to Structure Digital Stories

The structure of a story is like a garden path, a roller coaster, or good architecture: they are designed to be experienced over time and provide a variety of unique experiences along the way. We have to trust the designer to make the process interesting and emotionally vivid, with a conclusion that is rewarding or thought-provoking. Sometimes the story structure itself is an integral part of the information or reflects themes of a story, such as conveying a process of discovery or evoking frustration in the audience by withholding a definitive or satisfying ending (for topics about injustice, for example, or to help create a call to action in a PSA).

Consider these innovative ways to organize stories.

✦ **Raise a question.** Asked at the beginning or end of a story, questions add a layer of mystery and provoke the audience to go along for the ride to find out the answer.

✦ **Serialize.** Novels of the 19th century were often published as a series of chapters in magazines or newspapers. Consider this technique, embraced once again by streaming services, to tell long stories or create opportunities for collaborative storytelling. (Have each student or team create a post or "chapter" as part of a longer story series).

✦ **Withhold conclusions.** A risky choice is to avoid providing definitive answers for your audience. This doesn't mean that there isn't a conclusion to the story, but the ending either asks further questions or leaves the audience in such a state of investment in the topic that they are motivated to take action or continue the search for answers themselves. We see this often in PSAs or stories that have unfinished business that the audience has a responsibility for, like climate change, social justice, and civic duty. This also works for inspirational stories, where audiences may be motivated by a successful person or left wanting to try a creative or intellectual endeavor that is the focus of the story.

# Get Attention: Titles, Captions, and Taglines

Journalists and advertising executives know the power of headlines and slogans to attract audiences and help them remember a product. Titles, like a book cover or neon sign, get your audience's attention and can even help them discover your story online. Whether we like it or not, the headline or caption may be the only part of a story your audience ever reads, making it an essential part of the storytelling process that deserves our attention and creativity. I like to think of titles, headlines, and captions as the haiku of nonfiction storytelling.

## Titles

A good title can attract an audience through intrigue, novelty, surprise, or even straight-up directness. Titles should be brief, clever (but not too clever!), and specific. Use subtitles to add description. Here are some examples of effective titles for nonfiction stories.

✦ *A Brief History of Time* (Stephen Hawking): Using irony (time is not brief) to talk about the history of the universe.

+ *How to Win Friends and Influence People* (Dale Carnegie): Direct title that appeals to the audience's desires.

+ *How to Take over the World: Practical Schemes and Scientific Solutions for the Aspiring Supervillain* (Ryan North): Surprising and funny; the subtitle adds specifics.

+ *The Man Who Mistook His Wife for A Hat* (Oliver Sacks). Novel, surprising, and creates curiosity in the audience.

## Headlines

Headlines are used by newspapers and social media writers to attract attention, share the subject of their story, and set a mood or tone. They're different from titles of books or documentaries because they tend to be more literal and direct. Because headlines may also be the only part of a story your audience ever experiences, consider including names, statistics, and other facts.

Write headlines with search engine optimization (SEO) in mind. This means writing titles and headlines in a way that will help an audience find your story through online searches. Imagine that you're a member of your audience, then ask yourself, "What words or phrases would I search for if I were interested in this topic?" Include some of those words or phrases in the headline or title, including subtitles.

Tips for writing effective headlines:

+ Tell the story: describe what it is about, rather than being vague or overly clever.

+ Use action verbs.

+ Put the verb early in the headline.

+ Write in the active voice.

+ Write in the present or future tense.

| HEADLINE | WHY IT WORKS |
| --- | --- |
| "How an Ad Campaign Invented the Diamond Engagement Ring" (*The Atlantic*) | Explaining a phenomenon is a great way to attract audiences |
| "After Reaching Out His Hand, President Obama Will Step Foot in Cuba" (NPR) | Turns of phrase make this punny, but it also includes facts |
| "Ancient Tomb in Spain Is Destroyed and Replaced by Picnic Table" (NPR) | Clever without being too clever. Teases us with a novel situation that makes the audience want to find out more. |
| "Alabama Will Now Allow Yoga in Its Public Schools (But Students Can't Say 'Namaste')" (NPR) | Includes memorable details, and raises an unusual question we want to learn the answer to. |
| "Who's responsible for climate change? Three charts explain" (*MIT Technology Review*) | Direct and clear, it answers a question audiences have in their minds. |

**FIGURE 15.4 Attention getting:** *A well-phrased headline gets attention and includes key information.*

## Captions

Images like photographs, maps, videos, and data visualizations often need accompanying text to explain what we're looking at and provide information that is not visible in the image. Good captions are brief and avoid redundancy. (Don't describe what we can plainly see in the image.) It is also a way to cite sources, give credit to the creator of the image, or even add a brief story of a few sentences to provide context.

## Taglines

As we discussed in chapter 14 with the PSA project, taglines are a way for advertisers and other storytellers to create a memorable slogan that sticks with the audience, either to create brand recognition or to keep them thinking about the important ideas and information shared in your story. Good taglines should be catchy, memorable, and relate to the story topic or call to action. Use them at the end of a story like podcasts, explainers, and PSAs, or as graphics in social media stories.

Here are some examples of famous taglines. See if you can remember the brand.

✦ The Happiest Place on Earth

✦ A Diamond Is Forever

✦ The Ultimate Driving Machine

✦ Finger Lickin' Good

✦ Only You Can Prevent Wildfires

## Postscript on Writing Digital Stories

Digital stories are not visual essays—you shouldn't just write a traditional essay and add images to it. The success of student digital stories comes from letting go of traditional notions of what "writing" means, in terms of length, content, style, and distribution models, and embracing the strengths of other kinds of media to communicate to an audience in the most effective ways.

## Writing Tips

✦ **Shoot first, write later.** Record interviews and natural sound, snap photos, and create graphics first, then write in response to these data. Remember: the visual evidence of photos and video, and the testimony and natural sounds of audio are recorded in the effort to collect rich data. Any text (voiceovers, captions, etc.) should respond to the multimedia evidence in the same way a scientist writes their findings after concluding an experiment. Avoid using multimedia artifacts as ornamentation for written essays.

✦ **Show, don't tell.** What images or multimedia will you need to best communicate these concepts to not rely solely on text or voiceover?

✦ **Use repetition.** Text-based stories make it easy for a reader to quickly reread the previous paragraph if they missed something or need to dwell on a concept to understand it better, but this is much harder to do with time-based stories like podcasts or video. For multimedia stories like these, it's important to repeat definitions or data and provide cues and periodic brief summaries that remind the audience about how we got to this point in the story.

✦ **Use text strategically with multimedia.** Seeing and hearing data, facts, or definitions is extremely important for audience understanding, especially for numbers and statistics. In visual stories like photography and illustrations, include captions for value-added explanations. For videos, add titles on top of footage for increased clarity.

**FIGURE 15.5** *Writing as a way of thinking: Writing is at the heart of every digital story, from research, to scripts, to text that accompanies multimedia elements in digital books, websites, or social media posts. Using a workshop process assists the ideation process, elevates quality, and fosters a shared sense of purpose.*

# CHAPTER 16

# QUICK WIN PROJECTS TO TRY TOMORROW

This chapter is a list of projects that are easy to use and don't require a lot of time or training to complete. Have questions about using these projects in your learning space? Drop me a note at michael@storytelling-with-purpose.com.

## Me, Myselfie, and I

**Medium:** Photography

**Time to Complete:** 10–20 minutes

**Gear:** Smartphones or tablets with cameras

**The Project:** Have students use mobile devices to take a selfie photo as an introduction to the class.

**The Process:** Display the images either by projecting them on a screen or printing them out to post in your classroom. Have students look for patterns (composition, posing, etc.) as well as differences. Highlight those that use variety, innovation, and originality.

**The Point:** Use an easy, familiar process to learn how to discuss representation and our ability to discern image accuracy. Learn to describe details and draw conclusions from an image. Discover and celebrate difference and variety. Begin building a classroom culture of emotional safety and introduce how to give and receive feedback.

## The Story of You

**Medium:** Photography

**Time to Complete:** 20 minutes (plus time at home to take photos)

**Gear:** Smartphones or tablets with cameras

**The Project:** Students create a series of photos to introduce their life or worldview.

**The Process:** Have students create photos for each of four to five prompts, such as home, community, dream, fear, and passion. Students are free to interpret each theme as they wish. Arrange photos on a grid side by side with the rest of the class.

**The Point:** Practice photography skills while encouraging interpretation of themes. Get to know each other and everyone's worldview. Celebrate individuality, difference, and originality. Begin building a classroom culture of emotional safety and introduce how to give and receive feedback.

# Six-Shot Story

(This project was created by my friend Don Goble and used here with permission)

**Medium:** Photography or video

**Time to Complete:** 30–60 minutes (plus time outside of class to take photos or record video)

**Gear:** Smartphone or tablet with a camera

**The Project:** Students learn to tell a story using only six photos or six clips of video.

**The Process:** Students interpret a theme or prompt to record and arrange a photo or video story. Project student projects on screen for class critique, or embed on a website, digital book, or social media channel.

**The Point:** Practice photography and videography and learn video editing. Introduce story structure and sequencing and discuss how to give and receive feedback.

# Interview an Expert

**Medium:** Audio or video

**Time to Complete:** 30–60 minutes or more

**Gear:** Smartphone, tablet, or laptop with an audio recording app, or a video camera if recording video. Optional: external microphone

**The Project:** Students interview an expert on a topic of choice or related to a current project.

**The Process:** Identify the expert, write interview questions, and record the conversation. Publish the recording on a website, digital book, or social media channel. Optional: Edit the interview for clarity and length. Include all or part of this interview as part of a longer podcast project.

**The Point:** Practice the interview techniques like developing questions, scheduling, public speaking, and recording audio.

# Social Media Story

**Medium:** Social media

**Time to complete:** 30–60 minutes

**Gear:** Graphic design apps, social media account

**The Project:** Students create a three- to five-panel "carousel" social media post to explain a topic or share statistics gathered during research for a class project or larger story project.

**The Point:** Use social media as a storytelling medium to introduce basic design principles, develop a multimedia writing style, and discern the most important or relevant information for an audience.

# TOOLBOX FOR DIGITAL STORYTELLING

This section is a collection of tools used to create and publish stories, organized by both learning process and project. Because apps and tools for digital storytelling come and go and evolve, many of the resources discussed here tend to focus on general concepts rather than provide  a comprehensive list of specific tools or brands. Those that are specifically named here are trusted by many educators and storytellers. For my latest, updated recommendations, visit the online Digital Resources companion to this book, and follow the hashtag: #StorytellingWithPurpose. If you have suggestions for additions to this resource or need help figuring out how to use these tools, visit storytelling-with-purpose.com or drop me a note at michael@storytelling-with-purpose.com.

## Choosing the Right Tool for the Job

### Cost and Access

Many apps are free, but some are fee-based or are only available with one brand of digital ecosystem. An increasing number offer web-based versions, although typically with fewer features than their desktop or mobile versions. Education licenses are also available for free or much lower cost than their consumer versions, too, so be sure to check with software companies for details.

You can save money and training time by using apps that can be used for more than one storytelling technique. For example, Apple's Keynote (free) is much more than a presentation app—it can create graphics, record explainer videos, and even create sophisticated animations.

## What Gear to Buy

Not all technology is the same. Less expensive devices often have fewer features (such as high-quality cameras and microphones) and end up costing more in the end because of the need to purchase, store, and manage additional gear and apps. When investing in technology, consider the flexibility of the device to provide new opportunities for teaching and learning beyond your current needs, and their ability to support more sophisticated projects as you and your students become more confident and ambitious. As my friend Dr. Monica Burns explains in her book, *Tasks Before Apps*, capital investment in technology should always be based on curriculum.

# Tools by Process
## Tools for Brainstorming and Planning

Use these tools in all phases of production, including research and planning. These tools help students think, organize ideas, structure stories, plan the production process, and reflect on their work.

### IDEATION

+ Innovators' Compass (free). A design thinking tool and process that helps individuals or teams develop ideas and set goals.
+ Whiteboard apps like Mural, Explain Everything, Google Jamboard, and Apple Freeform allow teams to add and organize ideas similar to sticky notes on a whiteboard. Some allow students to draw and add multimedia elements like photos and video.

### JOURNALING AND WRITING

+ Capture ideas and take notes quickly with apps like Apple Notes, Notability, or Google Keep. Look for apps that allow students to capture media like photos, video, and audio, or allow handwriting and sketching (available on smartphones and tablets)
+ Word-processing apps like Pages, Word, or Google Docs for research, scripts, interview questions, and other writing needs for longer projects

### PLANNING

+ Spreadsheets like Google Sheets or Apple Numbers
+ Word processing apps like Google Docs or Apple Pages

## Tools for Team Communication

There is an evolving list of apps that allow teams to work together efficiently. Like professionals in the workplace, students may need to work independently outside of class time, when they can't be face-to-face, and when their work is timely (such as journalism projects or scientific research in the field). These tools are much more efficient than text groups because they allow for sharing of documents, can create calendar alerts, and provide a distinction between personal and professional spaces.

Some team communication apps include:

+ Slack
+ Microsoft Teams
+ Zoom

## Tools for Capturing Media

Recording visual and audio evidence is central to nonfiction digital storytelling. Use these apps to capture and document ideas, interviews, and phenomena.

- Camera. The native camera app on most smartphones and tablets works perfectly. Use paid apps to get more control and larger feature sets when you record, such as independently setting exposure and focus, or the ability to choose different recording formats.
- Microphone. The built-in mic on many smartphones or tablets should suffice. Get higher quality audio by using an external mic designed for recording interviews (lavalier mic) or sounds that originate far away, such as an animal in a tree (shotgun mic).

## Tools for Capturing Data

Polls and surveys are a great way to learn data collection and analysis skills, as well as how to develop good questions. The best analysis apps often require a subscription fee, but there are low-cost alternatives, depending on the level of sophistication you need. Look for apps that filter responses by specific criteria, make comparisons, or generate their own data visualizations.

Social media apps often include a simple poll feature, which can be a great way to engage your audience, but for more sophisticated data collection and analysis, choose a more sophisticated (and often fee-based) app.

Some polling and survey tools include:

- Google Forms
- Survey Monkey
- Slido
- Mentimeter

## Tools for Creating Data Visualizations

Create graphs and charts with tools like these. Look for tools that allow you to import CSV (spreadsheet) files.

- Keynote
- Excel
- Google Sheets
- Canva

## Tools for Creating Graphics

Create social media cards, titles for video stories, book covers, and editorial illustrations with these apps. Many are template-based, giving students a quick start when designing.

- Adobe Express
- Canva
- Presentation apps like Keynote or PowerPoint (which allow the export of still image formats as well as .gif animations and video)
- Procreate
- Adobe Photoshop
- Adobe Fresco

# Tools for Creating Animation

Animated sequences show movement and change, specifically for concepts we can't easily see or record with video or photography. Use them on their own, or within video stories like explainer videos, journalism, or documentary projects.

+ Keynote
+ PowerPoint
+ Adobe Fresco
+ Photoshop
+ Procreate
+ Stop Motion Studio
+ Life Lapse
+ Adobe After Effects (pro)
+ Apple Motion (pro)

# Tools for Editing Media

## PHOTO EDITING

Many native photography apps allow for basic adjustments like exposure (brightness), color, and cropping, and work well for most projects. When your students are ready, try more advanced tools like Adobe Photoshop or Fresco that allow for assemblage and collage techniques.

Look for features that allow:

+ adjustment of color, exposure, cropping
+ markup tools like drawing, text, and objects (for annotation)

+ advanced features like layers (multiple images that overlap or blend), selection of an area of an image, background removal, and the ability to export in different image formats, like .jpg, .pdf, or .gif.

## AUDIO EDITING

For podcasts and oral history projects, you'll need to trim and arrange audio clips, add voiceover, music, and sound effects, and mix these elements cohesively. Look for apps that allow you to adjust the volume of clips to bring quiet and loud recordings into alignment for a consistent sound level. Native apps have limited features, while professional paid apps can be sophisticated and unlock incredible features like looping and effects, filters, and advanced trimming and adjustment tools.

Popular audio editing apps include:

+ GarageBand
+ Soundtrap
+ Logic (pro app)
+ Adobe Audition (pro app)

## VIDEO EDITING

Like audio, video clips need to be trimmed, rearranged, and adjusted to create tight, economical stories that keep the audience engaged with good pacing. Look for apps that allow multiple tracks of video, create different aspect ratios (screen dimensions) to optimize for filmmaking and social media, and can export in different video formats. Free consumer apps are a snap to use but have limited features and lack the granularity and power of professional apps. Some tools even allow for cloud-based collaboration.

Popular video editing apps include:

✦ Apple Clips

✦ iMovie

✦ Adobe Express

✦ WeVideo (online)

✦ Final Cut Pro (pro)

✦ Adobe Premiere (pro)

✦ DaVinci Resolve (pro)

# Tools for Hosting and Distributing Stories

Once projects are complete, you'll want to share them with the world. Hosting stories online, either by using social media platforms like YouTube, or as a file upload to a cloud storage service, saves space on your local hard drive or server and allows you to share stories via links with students, parents, and administration. When students create digital books or portfolios that include multimedia stories, those portfolios can simply link to hosted video or audio stories rather than having to embed the actual media files, which keeps their book file sizes smaller. It's also a great way to archive projects so they don't get lost when devices or hard drives break.

## AUDIO

To share audio stories publicly, you'll want to host them (upload and store them) on a service that others can find and access. Podcast hosting services even push your shows out to major podcast sites like Spotify and Apple Podcasts to find international audiences, and provide analytics such as the number of times an episode has been played and what country your listeners live in. Some audio hosting services also provide online editing tools to make the process seamless. Top podcast and audio hosting services include Spotify for Podcasters, Soundcloud, and Podbean.

## VIDEO

YouTube and Vimeo are the most popular places to host videos, mostly because they are familiar and easy to use. Take advantage of the social aspect of these apps, which allows students to curate playlists that can be followed by an audience and allow for audience comments. Links to hosted videos can be shared on other stories such as social media posts and digital portfolios. Because video files are very large compared to audio, photography, or text files, hosting videos online saves space on your devices and hard drives.

## DIGITAL BOOKS

EPUB files generated by digital book publishing apps are similar to video or audio, in that they can be placed on your cloud storage service. A better option is to host books on an online service so that these stories can be found by an international audience, or when you want to charge a fee for your book. Services like Book Creator are already online and shareable, but for books created with apps on student devices, try services like Apple Books or Amazon. Even if you are making books available for free, you'll need to set up an account for tax purposes, so plan ahead.

**WEBSITES AND DIGITAL PORTFOLIOS**

There are many free design and hosting services students can use to create websites, from simple drag-and-drop templates to more complex designs based on open-source code like WordPress. Unless you're teaching a coding class where students create their sites from scratch, it's best to use template-based online services that allow drag-and-drop design. Look for services that:

✦ Allow upload of multimedia like photos, video, and audio

✦ Have user-friendly, customizable, drag-and-drop design tools

✦ Manage URL domain hosting

✦ For older students, I always recommend owning their own site outside of your school's domain or LMS. That way they can keep their portfolio once they change schools or graduate, encouraging true authentic ownership of their website.

# Tools Listed by Project

This section provides a quick reference for tools you'll need for storytelling projects outlined in part III. These are the basics of what you'll need to create each project, but you might decide to include additional tools to enhance a project, such as adding an animation to a documentary or infographics to a digital book. You should also expect to use some kind of brainstorming/writing/planning/communication tools in every project.

## Explainer Videos

✦ Presentation app, such as Keynote, PowerPoint, or Slides

Optional:

✦ Screen recording app (if not using Keynote)

✦ External microphone

✦ Data visualization or illustration apps

## Digital Books

✦ Apps that create/publish EPUB documents, such as Pages or other word processing app

✦ Online book publishing app, such as Book Creator

✦ E-reader app, like Apple Books (to test and review EPUB documents)

Optional:

✦ Graphic design tools to create cover images and other illustrations

## Audio Stories

✦ Audio recording app (for mobile devices), such as Voice Memos

✦ Audio recording app (for desktop devices), such as QuickTime, GarageBand, Soundtrap, or Zoom (for remote interviews)

✦ Audio editing app, such as GarageBand, Soundtrap, or pro apps like Logic or Audition

✦ Graphic design tools to create podcast logos and cover images

Optional:

- ✦ External microphone
- ✦ Podcast hosting service, such as Spotify for Podcasters, Podbean, Libsyn, or SoundCloud

## Video Documentaries

- ✦ Mobile device with video camera and microphone, or dedicated video camera
- ✦ Video editing software

Optional, but highly recommended:

- ✦ External microphone for interviews
- ✦ Tripod (for steady footage)

## Websites and Digital Portfolios

- ✦ Web design/hosting service
- ✦ Photo editing app (for cropping or adjusting images)
- ✦ Graphic design or illustration tool to create illustrations and cover images

## Social Media Stories

- ✦ Social media accounts
- ✦ Graphic design or illustration tool to create illustrations and cover images

## Graphic Novels

- ✦ Design or illustration app, such as Procreate or Adobe Fresco, Illustrator, or Photoshop. Or use free or low-cost tools like presentation apps and graphic organizers to create illustrations
- ✦ Digital book app, website, or social media account for publishing

# ETHICAL STORYTELLING

*We tell stories to build community, not to break it.*

**—Micaela Blei**

For me, the most important part of creating digital stories—even more than the curriculum we teach—is helping students understand the impact that their work has on others. Before they can use any of our curriculum or tell stories about it, they need to be clear on why they're doing so and anticipate what might happen when they do. Just because you *can* do something doesn't always mean you *should*.

In this section we share some mindsets and resources for developing ethical student storytellers. This is not intended to be a legal guide, but to spur further research on these topics by you and your students. Free speech rights vary by state and country, and new laws and court decisions can change the legal landscape continually, so be sure to check with legal experts when questions arise.

## Ethics of Storytelling
### Privacy

Privacy is the right to not be recorded or have one's personal information published or shared with others. But there are many gray areas and exceptions to this concept, and courts have determined that those rights vary depending on a person's age (young children vs. teens or adults), the location of a recording (a public space like schools and parks have less expectation of privacy than someone's home, for example), social status (private citizen vs. a public figure like a movie star or elected official), and intent (journalism compared to private gain like advertising).

There will be many times when finding clarity on this topic is difficult. Sometimes, the public's need to know (think health and safety, for example)

# Traits of an Ethical Storyteller

An ethical storyteller is someone who:

✦ Knows and understands one's legal free speech rights

✦ Develops personal and community-centered processes for how to make ethical decisions

✦ Creates stories thoughtfully and with generosity

✦ Is courageous and defends facts and the truth

✦ Provides transparency in their work

✦ Is respectful without being complicit or complacent

✦ Is open to feedback, corrections, and constructive criticism

outweighs the privacy of an individual or business. For example, when a company is polluting the environment, or an elected official embezzles funds or lies about their qualifications, sharing private information, including naming individuals, in documentaries or journalism stories is most often legal and ethical.

For most stories your students produce, privacy is a concept to discuss throughout the process. Often, it just means asking permission to record someone or their property. The more sophisticated the story project—like documentaries and investigative journalism—the more likely you are to encounter ethical dilemmas. Can you and your students justify why they need to include this person or facts?

## Copyright

It can be tempting for students and teachers to use music, images, or other media made by others, but in most cases this is actually illegal—it's like plagiarism for multimedia. The ability to use someone else's art, music, writing, images, or intellectual property is limited by copyright laws that automatically protect the ideas and effort of every content creator, including your students.

Understanding and teaching about copyright can prevent legal or financial repercussions and also model good digital citizenship. Despite the common myth, teachers and students are not exempt from copyright law just because we're using media for educational purposes. The only exceptions are when teachers use small clips of films or music to make a point in their lesson, or when short excerpts are used for journalistic purposes (such as a film or music review). But like all laws, copyright law evolves, and is different in each country.

The best way to avoid any legal or financial penalties for violating copyright law and to model good digital citizenship is to have students create their own work. But many organizations also make content available for public use, such as the National Gallery of Art in Washington, D.C., and the Metropolitan Museum of Art in New York. NASA also allows the use of its images. Every organization has its own usage rights policies, so be sure to check with them first.

In most cases, there is a distinction between commercial and non-commercial use of images and content. Commercial use means the media is used to make money, such as adding music or images for advertising, or in a film or music video. Non-commercial use typically covers scientific, journalistic, and academic use, such as the projects you and your students are most likely creating.

Royalty-free means that you may use media without paying a fee (a royalty) to the creator, although there may be restrictions on how you can use the work. Public domain means that the copyright on a work has expired, and anyone may use it for any purpose. Typically in the U.S., this means between 70 to 120 years after the death of the author or creator.

## Resources and Guidance for Legal and Ethical Storytelling

Rely on these resources to help guide your legal and ethical decision-making as students create storytelling projects.

**Student Press Law Center.** The SPLC is a nonprofit that supports journalism students and their advisers with free legal advice. Their website also has many resources that every teacher might find helpful, including the latest guidelines for copyright, privacy, libel, and slander, specifically as it relates to student digital storytellers.

**Creative Commons.** This international nonprofit provides licensing agreements and information about copyright, royalty-free media, and guidelines for how to use them. They also have a library of royalty-free media that anyone can use.

**U.S. Copyright Office.** For teachers working in the United States, this federal office provides the latest updates on copyright law and resources for using media made by others.

## Resources for Royalty-Free Media

Find royalty-free or public domain images, video, and audio with these resources. See the most current list of resources in the Digital Resources website.

+ Creative Commons
+ Unsplash
+ Canva (with free account)
+ Adobe Express (with free account)
+ YouTube (search for royalty-free video and music)

# How to Teach Privacy for Storytelling

To shift perspective and help students understand the concepts of public vs. private life and how to draw lines and become more ethical storytellers, I rely on one of the most ubiquitous digital stories of all: the selfie.

Using the "Me, Myselfie, and I" project from chapter 16, expand on the experience with an additional photo of each student taken by someone else in the class. Debrief with these discussion questions:

+ How was it different for you when someone else took your photo, rather than you taking a photo of yourself?

+ How did this new experience feel to you? Why?

+ What concerns do you have about this new photo, taken by your classmate? Why?

+ What would make you feel more comfortable when someone else takes your photo?

+ How might this experience change what you do when creating images or recordings of other people in your own projects?

# Modeling Ethical Storytelling

As teachers, it's important to practice what we preach. We, too, should use original works or royalty-free or public-domain images, video, and sound in our lessons and presentations. Take opportunities to point out privacy and copyright issues as they come up, and use media with the appropriate license in your own presentations. Model and point out proper citations for photos, video, and audio, just as you would for an academic paper.

# TEACHING AND LEARNING RESOURCES

Help drive your digital storytelling lessons further with the information and ideas from these books and other resources.

## Books

### Books about Teaching and Learning

*Tasks before Apps* by Dr. Monica Burns. Advice and examples for integrating technology in the classroom at every grade level.

*Teach Boldly: Using EdTech for Social Good* by Dr. Jennifer Williams. A practical guide to using tech to empower students so they can create positive change and develop a global mindset through the U.N.'s Sustainable Development Goals.

*Make Yourself Clear: How to Use a Teaching Mindset to Listen, Understand, Explain Everything, and Be Understood* by Reshan Richards and Stephen Valentine. With a mix of research, case studies, and theory, these education experts and entrepreneurs explain how to use digital tools to communicate effectively to achieve your goals and create meaningful interactions in an increasingly digital world.

## Books about Storytelling

*Everyone Can Create* by Apple. A series of free guides published by Apple that include lessons and projects for digital storytelling and creativity in all grade levels.

*Sound Reporting* by Jonathan Kern. Published by NPR, this is a detailed guide of writing and producing nonfiction audio stories.

*Understanding Comics* by Scott McCloud. Understand the unique narrative elements of graphic novels and how to exploit the medium to create original visual stories.

*Unflattening* by Nick Sousanis. A book about the nature of innovation, the relation of images and text, and how we understand the world and each other, created as a graphic novel.

*The Secret Language of Maps: How to Tell Visual Stories with Data* by Carissa Carter. A fun, accessible exploration of spatial and visual storytelling.

*Lies My Teacher Told Me: Everything Your American History Textbook Got Wrong* by James W. Loewen. A well-researched book that examines the intentional and accidental mistakes in U.S. history books.

*A People's History of the United States* by Howard Zinn. From Christopher Columbus until the 1990s, this book looks at U.S. history through the lens of women, people of color, and immigrants.

## Books about Creativity and Design

Learn the fundamentals of good design and layout with these resources.

*Intention: Critical Creativity in The Classroom* by Dan Ryder and Amy Burvall. These educators and design thinking experts share exercises, projects, and advice for developing critical thinking and a creative mindset.

*Steal Like an Artist* by Austin Kleon. Creative tips and exercises from artist and speaker Austin Kleon.

*Design Secrets Revealed* by Keri-Lee Beasley. This digital book covers the elements of design to help you create more effective graphics and layouts.

## Books by the Author

*Art of the Video Interview.* Learn videography, audio recording, sound editing, and how to develop interview questions. Includes exercises and sample projects.

*Creating Digital Books with Mac and iPad* (coauthored with Apple). Learn how to create and publish digital books with Apple's Pages app.

*Using Book Creator in the High School Classroom.* See the many ways teachers and administrators can use digital books to enhance teaching, learning, and community. See examples from educators around the world.

*Podcasting for the Classroom.* A detailed how-to guide to producing student podcasts. Hear examples and get insights from teachers around the world.

*Human Geography: A Digital Storytelling Project for Students and Teachers.* This book showcases a storytelling professional development experience designed and led by the author. See examples created by teachers and hear their reactions.

# Other Resources
## ISTE Standards

The International Society of Technology in Education (ISTE) as an organization is committed to serving and supporting global educators as they use technology to transform teaching and learning. The ISTE Standards are a framework to help educators and education leaders reengineer schools and classrooms for digital age learning.

Ideas shared in this book address the educator and student sections of the ISTE Standards. By their nature, storytelling projects are interdisciplinary, and each project covers many of the ISTE Standards at once. The way teachers decide to use the ideas in this book may also affect which standards are applied. For example, a student's self-reflection recorded as an audio file that is only heard by her teacher addresses fewer standards than if that recording is published publicly on the student's website and marketed to a wide audience through the use of an editorial illustration on social media. The beauty of the projects in this book is that they are flexible and customizable to accommodate the needs of every student and educator.

All projects address Student Standard 1.6 Creative Communicator and Educator Standards 2.5 Designer and 2.6 Facilitator. Below are the ISTE Standards for Students and Educators listed by steps of the storytelling process.

# The Art and Craft of Storytelling

National Geographic Education: Storytelling for Impact. These online courses walk you through how to create photos, video, graphics, and more.

The Moth. A nonprofit live storytelling event (and podcast) with free resources for educators.

StoryCorps. A nonprofit that records oral histories and archives them in the Library of Congress. See their website and mobile app for training and resources for recording audio interviews.

| STORYTELLING PROCESS | STUDENT STANDARDS | EDUCATOR STANDARDS |
|---|---|---|
| Research, ideation, story pitch | 1.3a, 1.3b, 1.5a, 1.5b, 1.5c, 1.7d | 2.3b, 2.4c, 2.4b, 2.5, 2.6a |
| Writing & planning | 1.3c, 1.3d, 1.4b, 1.4c | 2.4b, 2.5, 2.6a |
| Production | 1.4a, 1.4d, 1.7d | 2.4b, 2.5, 2.6b |
| Publishing and marketing | 1.2 (all) | 2.4c, 2.5, 2.6d, 2.7d |

Chapters that cover additional ISTE Standards:

| CHAPTER | STUDENT STANDARDS | EDUCATOR STANDARDS |
|---|---|---|
| 2.3 (Assessment) | 1.1c, 1.2a | 2.7 (all) |
| 3.5 (Advocacy) | 1.3d, 1.5b, 1.7d | 2.4d, |
| Appendix B (ethical storytelling) | 1.2 (all) | 2.3 (all) |

**FIGURE A.1 *ISTE Standards*** *If you need to provide evidence of how concepts in this book align with standards, use the ISTE Standards above. Read them in full at iste.org/standards.*

## Journalism

Join a network of experienced journalism educators and gain access to curriculum, training, and teacher forums with these scholastic journalism organizations.

✦ Journalism Education Association

✦ National Scholastic Press Association

✦ Columbia Scholastic Press Association

✦ Poynter Institute

✦ SchoolJournalism.org

## Accessibility, UDL, and Inclusiveness

*Mismatch: How Inclusion Shapes Design*, by Kat Holmes. A book for businesses and organizations that helps us see that clear, simplistic design for people of all abilities (signage, systems, presentations, etc.) is beneficial to everyone.

*Invisible Women: Data Bias in a World Designed for Men*, by Caroline Criado-Perez. Educators, scientists, businesses, and policy makers all rely on data to make decisions, develop products, evaluate people, and design systems. But it turns out, most data fails to account for women. This fascinating book provides case studies about gender bias in education, medicine, government, and more.

*Reach Everyone, Teach Everyone: Universal Design for Learning in Higher Education*, by Kirsten T. Behling and Thomas J. Tobin. It's often hard to understand how Universal Design for Learning applies to each of us in the classroom or faculty meeting. This book is filled with practical steps every teacher and administrator can take to lower barriers to learning for all students.

## Culture, Leadership, and Innovation

*Design For Belonging: How to Build Inclusion and Collaboration in Your Communities*, by Susie Wise (author) and Rose Jaffe (illustrator). Whether you're a classroom teacher or organizational leader, this book provides advice on how to create a culture of inclusiveness through a series of exercises and case studies.

*Elements of Leadership* by Apple. A step-by-step guide to help school leadership with innovation.

# BIBLIOGRAPHY/WORKS CITED

## Citations

**PROLOGUE**

Agarwal, P. K. (2019). Retrieval practice & Bloom's taxonomy: Do students need fact knowledge before higher order learning? *Journal of Educational Psychology, 111*(2), 189–209. https://doi.org/10.1037/edu0000282

CEW Georgetown University. (2019, May 15). *Born to win, schooled to lose: Why equally talented students don't get equal chances to be all they can be.* https://cew.georgetown.edu/cew-reports/schooled2lose/

Eschleman, K. J., Madsen, J., Alarcon, G., & Barelka, A. (2014). Benefiting from creative activity: The positive relationships between creative activity, recovery experiences, and performance-related outcomes. *Journal of Occupational and Organizational Psychology, 87*(3), 579–598. https://doi.org/10.1111/joop.12064

Kidd, C., & Hayden, B. Y. (2015). The psychology and neuroscience of curiosity. *Neuron, 88*(3), 449–460. https://doi.org/10.1016/j.neuron.2015.09.010

Marciano, J. (2001). Civic illiteracy and education: The battle for the hearts and minds of American youth. *Theory and Research in Social Education, 29*(3), 532–540. https://doi.org/10.1080/00933104.2001.10505955

Miller, S., & Pennycuff, L. (2008). The power of story: Using storytelling to improve literacy learning. *Journal of Cross-Disciplinary Perspectives in Education, 1*(1), 36–43. https://wmpeople.wm.edu/asset/index/mxtsch/storytelling

Shah, P. E., Weeks, H. M., Richards, B., & Kaciroti, N. (2018). Early childhood curiosity and kindergarten reading and math academic achievement. *Pediatric Research, 84*(3), 380–386. https://doi.org/10.1038/s41390-018-0039-3

Smith, P. L., Goodmon, L. B., Howard, J. R., Hancock, R., Hartzell, K. A., & Hilbert, S. E. (2019). Graphic novelisation effects on recognition abilities in students with dyslexia. *Journal of Graphic Novels and Comics, 12*(2), 127–144. https://doi.org/10.1080/21504857.2019.1635175

## CHAPTER 1

Crowley, K. & Jordan, M. (2019, June 24). *Base font effect on reading performance*. Readability Matters. https://readabilitymatters.org/articles/font-effect

Kalantzis, M. (2016). *Literacies* (2nd edition). Cambridge University Press.

## CHAPTER 2

Carter, C., & Stanford d.school. (2022). *The secret language of maps: How to tell visual stories with data.* Ten Speed Press.

## CHAPTER 4

Lu, J. G., Hafenbrack, A. C., Eastwick, P. W., Wang, D. J., Maddux, W. W., & Galinsky, D. (2017). Supplemental material for "Going out" of the box: Close intercultural friendships and romantic relationships spark creativity, workplace innovation, and entrepreneurship. *The Journal of Applied Psychology, 102*(7), 1091–1108. https://doi.org/10.1037/apl0000212.supp

## CHAPTER 5

Lu, J. G., Hafenbrack, A. C., Eastwick, P. W., Wang, D. J., Maddux, W. W., & Galinsky, A. D. (2017). "Going out" of the box: Close intercultural friendships and romantic relationships spark creativity, workplace innovation, and entrepreneurship. *Journal of Applied Psychology, 102*(7), 1091–1108. https://doi.org/10.1037/apl0000212

Whiting, K. (2020, October 21). *These are the top 10 job skills of tomorrow – and how long it takes to learn them*. World Economic Forum. https://www.weforum.org/agenda/2020/10/top-10-work-skills-of-tomorrow-how-long-it-takes-to-learn-them/

Wise, S., & Stanford d.school. (2022). *Design for belonging: How to build inclusion and collaboration in your communities*. Ten Speed Press.

## CHAPTER 7

Álvarez-Mendoza, I., Acle-Tomasini, G., & Lozada-García, R. (2018). Transforming outstanding potential in outstanding skills by using storytelling to develop intellectual abilities of gifted students at risk. *Creative Education, 09*(07), 1152–1167. https://doi.org/10.4236/ce.2018.97085

Lee, E., Hannafin, M.J. (2016). A design framework for enhancing engagement in student-centered learning: Own it, learn it, and share it. *Education Technology Research and Development, 64*(4), 707–734. https://doi.org/10.1007/s11423-015-9422-5

Saavedra, A. R., Liu, Y., Haderlein, S. K., Rapaport, A., Garland, M., Hoepfner, D., Morgan, K. L., & Hu, A. (2021). *Knowledge in action: Efficacy study over two years*. USC Center for Economic and Social Research. https://cesr.usc.edu/sites/default/files/Knowledge%20in%20Action%20Efficacy%20 Study_18feb2021_final.pdf

## CHAPTER 8

Gruber, M. J., Gelman, B. D., & Ranganath, C. (2014). States of curiosity modulate hippocampus-dependent learning via the dopaminergic circuit. *Neuron, 84*(2), 486–496. https://doi.org/10.1016/j .neuron.2014.08.060

Koparan, T., & Guven, B. (2014). The effect of project based learning on the statistical literacy levels of student 8th grade. *European Journal of Educational Research, 3*(3), 145–157. https://doi.org/10.12973 /eu-jer.3.3.145

Lehne, M., Engel, P., Rohrmeier, M., Menninghaus, W., Jacobs, A. M., & Koelsch, S. (2015). Reading a suspenseful literary text activates brain areas related to social cognition and predictive inference. *PLOS ONE, 10*(5). https://doi.org/10.1371/journal.pone.0124550

McLeish, T. (2019). *The poetry and music of science: Comparing creativity in science and art* (Illustrated edition). Oxford University Press.

Summers, E. J., & Dickinson, G. (2012). A longitudinal investigation of project–based instruction and student achievement in high school social studies. *Interdisciplinary Journal of Problem-Based Learning, 6*(1). https://doi.org/10.7771/1541-5015.1313

## CHAPTER 9

Marzano, R. J. (2009*). The art and science of teaching / when students track their progress*. ASCD. https://www.ascd.org/el/articles/when-students-track-their-progress

# INDEX

Index

Index

Index

# IF YOU LIKED THIS BOOK, CHECK OUT THESE GREAT ISTE TITLES!

**All books available in print and ebook formats at iste.org/books**

## Moviemaking in the Classroom:
### Lifting Student Voices Through Digital Storytelling
**BY JESSICA PACK**

Written by an award-winning classroom teacher, this book offers quick-start lesson plans for any content area and grade level, helping students amplify their voices and effect change through moviemaking.

**iste.org/Moviemaking**

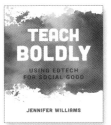

## Teach Boldly: Using Edtech for Social Good
**BY JENNIFER WILLIAMS**

Transformational education leader Jennifer Williams offers design- and empathy-driven practices to help teachers activate positive change in student learning.

**iste.org/TeachBoldly**

## New Realms for Writing: Inspire Student Expression With Digital Age Formats
**BY MICHELE HAIKEN**

Boost students' communication and writing skills, with strategies and examples to help them craft their own stories, tell their truth and be heard.

**iste.org/WritingRealms**

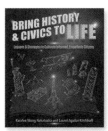

## Bring History and Civics to Life:
### Lessons and Strategies to Cultivate Informed, Empathetic Citizens
**BY KARALEE WONG NAKATSUKA AND LAUREL AGUILAR-KIRCHHOFF**

This user-friendly guide will empower and equip teachers to take a fun, interactive approach to using technology to teach history and civics.

**iste.org/History2Life**